THE COMPLETE BOOK OF

ITALIAN COOKING

THE COMPLETE BOOK OF

ITALIAN COOKING

Edited by
Veronica Sperling & Christine McFadden

PARRAGON

First published in Great Britain in 1996 by
Parragon Book Service Ltd
Unit 13–17
Avonbridge Trading Estate
Atlantic Road
Avonmouth
Bristol BS11 9QD

ISBN: 0-75252-058-X

Printed in Italy

Produced by Haldane Mason, London

Acknowledgements
Art Direction: Ron Samuels
Design: Digital Artworks Partnership Ltd

Material contained in this book has previously appeared in
Italian Farmhouse Cooking by Judy Bugg
Italian Regional Cooking and *Soups & Broths* by Rosemary Wadey
Pasta Dishes by Pamela Westland
Pizzas by Wendy Lee
Sensational Salads by Carole Handslip
Vegetarian Main Meals by Kathryn Hawkins
Additional recipes by Kathryn Hawkins

Contents

INTRODUCTION 6

ANTIPASTI &
ACCOMPANIMENTS 18

SOUPS 46

PASTA DISHES 60

FISH DISHES 122

POULTRY &
MEAT DISHES 136

RICE, POLENTA
& GNOCCHI 168

PIZZAS 184

DESSERTS 240

INDEX 254

ITALIAN CUISINE

Tourists flock in their millions to Italy, drawn by the ancient Roman architecture, the wealth of art galleries and churches, the famous Renaissance paintings and carefully restored frescos by Michelangelo on the ceiling and walls of the Sistine Chapel in the Vatican, Rome. They also go to enjoy the warm, friendly atmosphere and the food!

A CULINARY HISTORY

The Italian cuisine that we know today is the result of a very chequered history. Over the centuries, many different races from all over Europe invaded or travelled through the Italian peninsula bringing with them new culinary ideas. The Etruscans brought polenta and the Greeks introduced wonderful seafood cookery. The Romans not only developed the Greek style of cookery but wrote down their recipes – and they still exist today.

In 1861, the Unification of Italy brought twenty separate provinces under one flag, but the different regional styles of cooking remained largely unchanged.

ITALIAN FOOD REGION BY REGION

The most significant divide for Italy's cuisine is that between the industrial north and the poorer south. The north, with its fertile plains, its mountains and lakes, produces good quality wines and dairy foods. By contrast, the sunnier, rockier south is home to olive groves, aubergines (eggplant), tomatoes and herbs. Although there are regional differences in the cuisine, they do have features in common: the ingredients are fresh, techniques are simple, recipes are traditional and cooking, even in restaurants, is home-style.

Piedmont

The name means 'at the foot of the mountain', which it is, bordering on both France and Switzerland. Its fertile arable fields are irrigated by the many canals which flow through the region.

The food is substantial, peasant-type fare, though the wildly expensive fragrant white truffle is found in this region. Truffles are finely flaked or grated and added to many of the more sophisticated dishes. There is an abundance of wild mushrooms and a wide variety of game. Garlic features strongly in the recipes and polenta, gnocchi and rice are eaten in larger quantities than pasta, the former being offered as a first course when soup is not served.

Lombardy

The mention of Milan, the capital of the province, produces immediate thoughts of the wonderful risotto named after the city and also the Milanese soufflé flavoured strongly with lemon. Veal dishes, including *vitello tonnato* and *osso buco*, are specialities of the region and other excellent meat dishes, particularly pot roasts, feature widely.

The lakes of the area produce a wealth of fresh fish. Rice and polenta are popular but pasta also appears in many guises. The famous sweet yeasted cake panettone is a delicious product of this region.

Trentino-Alto Adige

This is an area of mountains, rich green valleys and lakes where fish are plentiful. There is a strong German influence, particularly when it comes to the wines. There are also several German-style liqueurs produced, such as Aquavit, Kümmel and Slivovitz.

The foods are robust and basic. Pasta as well as simple meat and offal dishes are popular, particularly in the Trentino area. In the Adige, soups and pot roasts are favoured, often with added dumplings and spiced sausages.

Veneto

The cooking in this north-east corner is straightforward, with generous portions of polenta served with almost everything. The land is intensively farmed, providing mostly cereals and wine. Pasta is less in evidence, with polenta, gnocchi

and rice more favoured. Fish is in abundance and especially good seafood salads are widely available. There are also excellent robust soups and risottos flavoured with the seafood and sausages of the area.

LIGURIA

The Genoese are excellent cooks, and all along the Italian Riviera can be found excellent trattorias which produce amazing fish dishes flavoured with the local olive oil. Pesto sauce flavoured with basil, cheese and pine kernels (nuts) comes from this area, along with other excellent sauces. Fresh herbs are widely used in many dishes including the famous pizzas – their aroma is unmistakable.

EMILIA-ROMAGNA

This is a special region of gastronomic excellence characterized by an abundance of rich food. Tortellini and lasagne are among the many pasta dishes which feature widely, as do *saltimbocca* and other veal dishes. Parma is famous for its ham, *prosciutto di Parma*, thought to be the best in the world. Modena ia famous for balsamic vinegar, which has grown in popularity over the past decade. The vinegar is distilled from wine until it becomes dark brown and develops an extremely rich flavour.

TUSCANY

The Tuscans share the Emilians great pride in cooking and eating, and are known to have hefty appetites. Tuscany has everything: an excellent coastal area providing splendid fish, hills covered in vineyards and fertile plains where every conceivable vegetable and fruit happily grow. There is plenty of game in the region, providing many interesting recipes. Tripe cooked in a thick tomato sauce is popular, as well as many liver dishes. Beans appear frequently in many guises, and there are richly flavoured pot roasts, steaks and full-bodied soups. Florence boasts a wide variety of specialities such as the hefty chargrilled T-bone steak *bistecca alla Fiorentina*, while Siena is the home of the famous candied spiced fruit cake *panforte di Siena*.

UMBRIA/MARCHES

Although not especially spectacular, the cuisine of inland Umbria is noted for its pork and the use of local fresh ingredients of excellent quality. These include lamb, game and freshwater fish from the lakes. Spit-roasting and grilling are popular, and the excellent local olive oil is used both in cooking and to pour over dishes before serving. Black truffles, olives, fruit and herbs are plentiful and feature in many recipes. Eastwards to the Marches, the food tends to be more elaborate with almost every restaurant noted for its excellent cuisine. The wealth of fish from the coast adds to the variety as do first-class sausages and cured pork. Pasta features widely all over the region.

LAZIO

Rome is the capital of both Lazio and Italy, and thus has become a focal point for specialities from all over the country. The cooking is characterized by robust flavours and rich sauces, but dishes tend to be fairly simple and quick to prepare, hence the many pasta dishes with delicious sauces, and gnocchi in various forms. There are also plenty of dishes featuring lamb, veal (*saltimbocca* being just one) and offal, all with generous amounts of herbs and seasonings. Vegetables and fantastic fruits are always in abundance in the local markets; and beans appear in soups and many other dishes.

ABRUZZI AND MOLISE

Formerly counted as just one region called Abruzzi e Molise, these regions have a mountainous interior with river valleys, high plateaux, densely forested areas and a coastal plain. The cuisine here is deeply traditional, with local hams and cheeses from the mountain areas, interesting sausages with plenty of garlic and other seasonings, cured meats, and wonderful fish and seafood. Lamb features widely: tender, juicy and well-flavoured with herbs.

CAMPANIA

Naples is the home of pasta dishes, served with a splendid tomato sauce (with many variations) famous worldwide. Pizza is said to have been created in Naples and now has spread to the north of the country and indeed all over the world.
Fish abounds, with *fritto misto* and *fritto pesce* being great favourites, varying daily depending on the catch. Fish stews are robust and varied, and shellfish in particular is often served with pasta. Cutlets and steaks are excellent, served with strong sauces usually flavoured with garlic, tomatoes and

herbs: pizzaiola steak is one of the favourites. Excellent mozzarella cheese is produced locally and used to create the crispy *mozzarella in carozza*, again served with a garlicky tomato sauce. Sweet dishes are popular too, often with flaky pastry and ricotta cheese, and the seasonal fruit salads laced with wine or liqueur take a lot of beating.

Puglia (Apulia)

The ground is stony but it produces good fruit, olives, vegetables and herbs, and, of course, there is a large amount of seafood. Puglians are said to be champion pasta eaters: many of the excellent pasta dishes are exclusive to the region both in shape and ingredients. Mushrooms abound and are always added to the local pizzas.

Oysters and mussels are plentiful, and so is octopus. Brindisi is famous for its shellfish – both the seafood salads and risottos are truly memorable. But it is not all fish or pasta: lamb is roasted or stewed to perfection and so is veal, always with plenty of herbs.

Basilicata

This is a sheep-farming area, mainly mountainous, where potent wines are produced to accompany a robust cuisine largely based on pasta, lamb, pork, game and abundant dairy produce. The salamis and cured meats are excellent, as are the mountain hams. Lamb is flavoured with the herbs and grasses on which it feeds. Wonderful thick soups – true minestrone – are produced in the mountains, and eels and fish are plentiful in the lakes.

Chilli peppers are grown in this region and appear in many of the recipes. They are not overpoweringly strong, although the flavours of the region in general tend to be quite strong and intense. The cheeses are excellent, good fruit is grown and interesting local bread is baked in huge loaves.

Calabria

This is the toe of Italy, where orange and lemon groves flourish along with olive trees and a profusion of vegetables, especially aubergines (eggplant) which are cooked in a variety of ways.

Chicken, rabbit and guinea fowl are often on the menu, as are pizzas, often with a fishy topping. Mushrooms grow well in the Calabrian climate and feature in many dishes from sauces and stews to salads. Pasta comes with a great variety of sauces including baby artichokes, eggs, meat, cheese, mixed vegetables, the large sweet (bell) peppers of the region and of course garlic. The fish is excellent too, with fresh tuna and swordfish available, as well as many other varieties.

Like most southern Italians, the Calabrians are sweet-toothed. Many desserts and cakes are flavoured with aniseed, honey, almonds and the plentiful figs of the region.

Sicily

This is the largest island in the Mediterranean and the cuisine is based mainly on fish and vegetables. Fish soups, stews and salads appear in unlimited forms, including tuna, swordfish, mussels and many more. Citrus fruits are widely grown as well as almonds and pistachio nuts. The local wines, including the dark, sweet dessert wine Marsala, are excellent.

Meat is often given a long, slow cooking, or else is minced (ground) and shaped before cooking. Game is plentiful and is often cooked in sweet-sour sauces containing the local black olives. Pasta abounds again, with more unusual sauces as well as the old favourites.

All Sicilians have a love of desserts, cakes and especially ice-cream. Cassata and other ice-creams from Sicily are famous all over the world, and the huge variety of flavours of both ice creams and granita makes it difficult to decide which is your favourite.

Sardinia

A pretty island with a wealth of flowers in the spring, but the landscape dries out in the summer from the hot sun. The national dish is suckling pig or newborn lamb cooked on an open fire or spit. Rabbit, game and offal dishes are also very popular. Fish is top quality, with excellent sea bass, lobsters, tuna, mullet, eels and mussels in good supply.

The sweet dishes are numerous and often extremely delicate, and for non-sweet eaters there is fresh fruit of almost every kind in abundance.

The island has a haunting aroma which drifts from many kitchens. It is myrtle (*mirto*), a local herb which is added to anything and everything from chicken to the local liqueur. Along with the wonderful cakes and breads of Sardinia, myrtle will long remain a memory of the island when you have returned home.

GETTING TO KNOW PASTA

Many of the popular pasta dishes have their origins in Italy where pasta has been produced since the thirteenth century or earlier. The word pasta simply means 'paste' or 'dough' in Italian.
The principal ingredients of traditional pasta are modest, although today there are more and more types of fresh and dried pasta available. By far the most popular type is made from durum wheat, which is milled to form fine semolina grains and then extruded through drums fitted with specially perforated discs, producing an estimated 600 different pasta varieties.

VARIETIES OF PASTA

Pasta is made from either the endosperm of wheat, or from the whole wheat grain, which contains more dietary fibre. The addition of spinach paste produces an attractive green colour – *lasagne verde* is a popular example; tomato purée (paste) produces a deep coral colouring.

As well as green and red pasta, there are other colours available: saffron pasta is an attractive yellow-orange colour, beetroot-hued pasta is a deep pink, and pasta coloured with squid ink is a dramatic black which makes any dish truly eye-catching. You can also buy or make pasta flecked with chopped basil or other herbs. *Pasta all'uovo*, made with eggs, is a rich yellow and produced in a range of shapes, both fresh and dried. Pasta is also made from ground buckwheat which gives the product a greyish colour and nutty flavour that combines well with vegetable and herb sauces.

Apart from these refinements of colour and flavour, pasta is generally divided into four main categories: long and round pasta, ribbons, tubes and shapes. Since dried pasta has a shelf life of up to six months (page 12) and fresh pasta may be frozen for up to six months, it is a good idea to build up your own selection of varieties with which to surprise your family and friends.

The following is a glossary of some of the different types of pasta:

ANELLI, ANELLINI small rings used for soup

BOZZOLI deeply-ridged, cocoon-like shapes

BUCATINI long, medium-thick tubes

CAPPELLETTI wide-brimmed hat shapes

CAPPELLI D'ANGELO 'angel's hair', thinner than cappellini

CAPPELLINI fine strands of ribbon pasta

CASARECCIA short curled lengths of pasta twisted at one end

CAVATAPPI short, thick corkscrew shapes

CONCHIGLIE ridged shells

CONCHIGLIETTE little shells used for soup

CORNETTI ridged shells

CRESTI DI GALLO curved shapes

DITALI, DITALINI short tubes

ELICHE loose spiral shapes

ELICOIDALI short, ridged tubes

FARFALLE bows

FEDELI, FEDELINI fine tubes twisted into 'skeins'

FESTONATI short lengths, like garlands

FETTUCCINE ribbon pasta, narrower than tagliatelle

FIOCHETTE, FIOCHELLI small bow shapes

FREZINE broad, flat ribbons

FUSILLI spindles, or short spirals

FUSILLI BUCATI thin spirals, like springs

GEMELLI 'twins', two pieces wrapped together

GRAMIGNA meaning 'grass' or 'weed'; the shapes look like sprouting seeds

LASAGNE flat, rectangular sheets

LINGUINI long, flat ribbons

LUMACHE smooth, snail-like shells, good with seafood sauces

LUMACHINE U-shaped flat noodles

MACARONI, MACCHERONI long or short-cut tubes, may be ridged or elbow-shaped

MALTAGLIATI triangular-shaped pieces, traditionally used in bean soups

ORECCHIETTE dished ear shapes

ORZI tiny rice-like grains used in soups

PAPPARDELLE widest ribbons, either straight or sawtooth-edged

PEARLINI tiny discs

PENNE short, thick tubes with diagonal-cut ends

PIPE RIGATE ridged, curved pipe shapes

RIGATONI thick, ridged tubes

RUOTI wheels

SEMINI seed shapes

SPAGHETTI fine, medium or thick rods

SPIRALE two rods twisted into spirals

STROZZAPRETI 'priest strangler', double twisted strands

TAGLIARINI flat ribbon, thinner than tagliatelle

TAGLIATELLE broad, flat ribbons

TORTIGLIONE thin, twisted tubes

VERMICELLI fine, slender strands usually sold folded into 'skeins'

ZITI TAGLIATI short, thick tubes

NUTRITIONAL VALUE OF PASTA

Pasta has frequently had to answer to the charge that it is a fattening food which must be be avoided by anyone who is on a weight-reducing diet. The answer to that charge is that it may not be the pasta that piles on the calories, but more likely some of the sauces we choose to serve with it.

This table shows you some of the dietary and nutritional credentials of dry uncooked pasta.

	per 100g
Protein	12.0g
Fat	1.8g
Dietary fibre	5.1g
Carbohydrate	74.1g
Calories	342

Basic Pasta Dough

Making your own pasta dough is time consuming but immensely satisfying. You will need plenty of space for the rolled-out dough, and somewhere to hang it to dry. Serves four.

125 g/4 oz/1 cup strong plain (all-purpose) flour,
plus extra for dusting
125 g/4 oz/²⁄₃ cup fine semolina
1 tsp salt
2 tbsp olive oil
2 eggs
2–3 tbsp hot water

Sieve the flour, semolina and salt into a bowl and make a well in the centre. Pour in half the oil and add the eggs. Add 1 tablespoon of hot water and, using your fingertips, work to a smooth dough. Sprinkle on a little more water if necessary to make the dough pliable.

Lightly dust a board with flour, turn the dough out and knead it until it is elastic and silky. This could take 10–15 minutes. Dust the dough with more flour if your fingers become sticky.

Alternatively, put the eggs, 1 tablespoon hot water and the oil in the bowl of a food processor and process for a few seconds. Add the flour, semolina and salt and process until smooth. Sprinkle on a little more hot water if necessary to make the dough pliable. Transfer to an electric mixer and knead using the dough hook for 2–3 minutes.

Divide the dough into two equal pieces. Cover a work surface (counter) with a clean cloth or tea towel (dish cloth) and dust it liberally with flour. Place one portion of the dough on the floured cloth and roll it out as thinly and evenly as possible, stretching the dough gently until the pattern of the weave shows through. Cover it with a cloth and roll out the second piece in a similar way.

Use a ruler and a sharp knife blade to cut long, thin strips for noodles, or small confectionery cutters to cut rounds, stars or other decorative shapes.

Cover the dough shapes with a clean cloth and leave them in a cool place (not the refrigerator) for 30–45 minutes to become partly dry. To dry ribbons, place a tea towel (dish cloth) over the back of a chair and hang the ribbons over it.

Pasta machines

If you get caught up in the enthusiasm of pasta making, you might like to buy a machine to roll, stretch and cut the dough. The method is to feed the pasta repeatedly through the rollers one notch thinner each time. This is time-consuming but important, as the pasta needs to keep its elasticity.

To roll the pasta from the Basic Pasta Dough recipe (page 11), first divide the dough into two pieces. Roll until all the pieces have gone through the machine at each setting. If the strips become too long and unwieldy, cut them into managable lengths.

Lay the pasta out on tea towels (dish cloths) to dry until it feels leathery, which is when it is ready to be cut. The machine will cut pasta into strips for ribbon pasta; other shapes will have to be cut by hand. Place a tea towel (dish cloth) over the back of a chair and hang the strips to dry, then use immediately.

Cooking pasta

The real enjoyment of pasta depends upon the cooking time. Undercooked, it will be unyielding and taste of raw flour; overcooked, it will be soft and sticky. The Italians describe the perfect texture as *al dente*, meaning that the pasta is tender but still slightly resistant to the bite.

Cooking times vary according to the type and volume of the pasta, and you should always follow the times recommended on the packet. In general, fresh pasta will be cooked in 3–5 minutes; dried pasta in 6–7 minutes for fine strands such as vermicelli; 7–12 minutes for quick-cooking macaroni, spaghetti and noodles; and 10–15 minutes for cannelloni tubes and sheets of lasagne.

Whatever the pasta type, have ready a large pan of water at a steady, rolling boil. Add salt and 1 tablespoon of olive oil to prevent sticking. Add the pasta gradually, a handful or a few strands at a time so that the water continues to boil and the pasta is kept separate. Do not completely cover the pan, or the water will boil over. Leave it uncovered, or partly covered. Drain the cooked pasta into a colander and, if it is not to be served at once, return it to the pan with a little olive oil.

How much to allow

It is difficult to calculate exactly how much pasta to allow for each serving. For a first course or salad, 40–50 g/1–2 oz dried pasta per person is about right, and 75–100 g/3–4 oz dried pasta for a main dish. It is worth remembering that dried pasta more than doubles in volume during cooking, absorbing water until it is rehydrated. Fresh pasta will not absorb so much.

Storing and freezing pasta

Dried pasta will keep in good condition for up to six months. Keep it in the packet, and reseal it once you have opened it, or transfer the pasta to an airtight jar.

Fresh pasta has a very short storage life, only one or two days in the refrigerator, so buy it only when you want to serve it. Otherwise it can be frozen for up to six months.

Cooked pasta may be stored for up to three days in the refrigerator. If the pieces have stuck together, turn them in a colander and run warm water through them. Drain well, then toss the pasta in hot olive oil or melted butter before serving. Cooked pasta may be frozen for up to three months but must be thawed at room temperature before reheating.

PASTA SAUCES

Creative cooks will enjoy partnering their favourite sauces with a variety of pastas. Although there are classic combinations such as Spaghetti Bolognese and Spaghetti Carbonara, there are no rules, just guidelines which are largely a matter of practicality, appearance and taste. For example, long ribbons or round pasta gives tomato- or oil-based sauces something to cling to, while shapes and hollow tubes are ideal for trapping chunkier sauces in their crevices. Béchamel and cheese sauces add creamy richness and moisture to baked pasta dishes.

Basic Tomato Sauce

2 tbsp olive oil
1 small onion, chopped
1 garlic clove, chopped
425 g/14 oz can chopped tomatoes
2 tbsp chopped parsley
1 tsp dried oregano
2 bay leaves
2 tbsp tomato purée (paste)
1 tsp sugar
salt and pepper

Heat the oil in a pan over a medium heat and fry the onion until translucent. Add the garlic and fry for another minute.

Stir in the chopped tomatoes, parsley, oregano, bay leaves, tomato purée (paste), sugar, and salt and pepper.

Bring the sauce to the boil, then simmer, uncovered, for 15–20 minutes until the sauce has reduced by half. Taste the sauce and adjust the seasoning if necessary. Discard the bay leaves before serving.

Béchamel Sauce

300 ml/½ pint/1¼ cups milk
2 bay leaves
3 cloves
1 small onion
60 g/2 oz/¼ cup butter, plus extra for greasing
45 g/1½ oz/6 tbsp flour
300 ml/½ pint/1¼ cups single (light) cream
large pinch of freshly grated nutmeg
salt and pepper

Pour the milk into a small pan and add the bay leaves. Press the cloves into the onion, add to the pan and bring the milk to the boil. Remove from the heat and set it aside to cool.

Strain the milk into a jug and rinse the pan. Melt the butter in the pan and stir in the flour. Stir for 1 minute, then gradually pour on the milk, stirring constantly. Cook the sauce for 3 minutes, then pour on the cream and bring it to the boil Remove from the heat and season to taste with nutmeg, salt and pepper.

Lamb Sauce

2 tbsp olive oil
1 large onion, sliced
2 celery stalks, thinly sliced
500 g/1 lb lean lamb, minced (ground)
3 tbsp tomato purée (paste)
150 g/5 oz bottled sun-dried tomatoes, drained and chopped
1 tsp dried oregano
1 tbsp red wine vinegar
150 ml/¼ pint/⅔ cup chicken stock
salt and pepper

Heat the oil in a frying pan over a medium heat and fry the onion and celery until the onion is translucent. Add the lamb and fry, stirring frequently, until it browns.

Stir in the tomato purée, sun-dried tomatoes, oregano, vinegar and stock. Season with salt and pepper.

Bring to the boil and cook, uncovered, for 20 minutes or until the meat has absorbed the stock. Taste and adjust the seasoning if necessary.

Cheese Sauce

30 g/1 oz/2 tbsp butter
1 tbsp flour
250 ml/8 fl oz/1 cup milk
2 tbsp single (light) cream
pinch of freshly grated nutmeg
salt and pepper
45 g/1½ oz mature (sharp) Cheddar, grated
1 tbsp freshly grated Parmesan

Melt the butter in a pan, stir in the flour and cook for 1 minute. Gradually pour on the milk, stirring all the time. Stir in the cream and season the sauce with nutmeg, salt and pepper.

Simmer the sauce for 5 minutes to reduce, then remove it from the heat and stir in the cheeses. Stir until the cheeses have melted and blended into the sauce.

Italian cheeses for pasta

Some cheeses have a natural affinity with pasta dishes and appear frequently in recipes.

RICOTTA A milky white, soft and crumbly Italian cheese similar to cottage cheese. It is low in fat, being made from whey, but some varieties produced now have whole milk added. If you cannot obtain Ricotta, use another low-fat soft cheese. To obtain a smooth-textured sauce or filling press through a sieve.

PARMESAN A mature and exceptionally hard cheese, Parmesan is the most important of flavourings for pasta. It may be useful to have a small carton of ready-grated Parmesan in the refrigerator, but you will find that it quickly loses its pungency and 'bite'. For that reason, it is better to buy small quantities of the cheese in one piece and grate it yourself. Tightly wrapped in clingfilm and foil, it can be kept in the refrigerator for several months. Grate it just before serving, for maximum flavour.

PECORINO A hard sheep's milk cheese which resembles Parmesan and is often used for grating over dishes. It has a sharp flavour and is only used in small quantities.

MOZZARELLA Another highly popular cheese, this is a soft cheese, with a bland flavour, traditionally made from water buffalo's milk. Buffalo's milk is now scarce, and so this cheese is often made with cow's milk. It can be used fresh, most popularly in salads, and also provides a tangy layer in baked dishes or a topping for pizzas.

Olive oil

Olive oil, which is at the heart of so many Italian dishes, has a personality all of its own, and each variety has its own characteristic flavour.

EXTRA-VIRGIN OLIVE OIL This is the finest grade, made from the first, cold pressing of hand gathered olives. Always use extra-virgin oil for salad dressings.

VIRGIN OLIVE OIL This oil has a fine aroma and colour, and is also made by cold pressing. It may have a slightly higher acidity level than extra-virgin oil.

REFINED OLIVE OIL This is made by treating the paste residue from the pressings with heat or solvents to extract the residual oil.

OLIVE OIL OR PURE OLIVE OIL This is a blend of refined and virgin olive oil.

GETTING TO KNOW PIZZAS

The pizza has become a universally popular food, in every form from the genuine article – thin, crisp and oven-baked – to frozen and fast-food pizza slices. The delightful aroma of freshly baked pizza topped with tomatoes, fresh herbs and cheese rarely fails to have a mouthwatering effect.

History of the Pizza

Although there is much speculation about where pizza in its simplest form was first invented, it is usually associated with the old Italian city of Naples. It was then a simple street food, richly flavoured and quickly made. It was not always round and flat as we know it today, but was originally folded up like a book, with the filling inside, and eaten by hand. Pizzas were usually sold on the streets by street criers who carried them around in copper cylindrical drums kept hot by coals from the pizza ovens.

The word 'pizza' actually means any kind of pie. The classic Napoletana pizza is probably the best-known of the many varieties. This consists of a thin crust of dough topped simply with a fresh tomato sauce, Mozzarella cheese, olives, anchovies and a sprinkling of oregano. When baked, the flavours blend perfectly together to give the distinctive aromatic pizza. Another classic is the 'Margherita' pizza, named after the Italian Queen Margherita. Bored with the usual cuisine when on a visit to Naples, she asked to sample a local speciality. The local 'Pizzaiolo' created a pizza in the colours of the Italian flag – red tomatoes, green basil and white Mozzarella. The Queen was delighted, and it became widely celebrated.

As well as being economical and popular, few other dishes are as versatile as the pizza, thanks to the countless possible permutations of bases and toppings that can be served to suit every palate and every occasion.

Fortunately for the busy cook, pizzas are an easy food to chill or freeze, ready to be cooked on demand. There is a wide range of ready-made pizza bases as well as dry mixes which only need the addition of water before they are ready for kneading and baking.

Pizzas are also sold complete with a variety of toppings, which you can bake as they are, or add more toppings yourself. Although they never seem to taste as good as a real homemade pizza, these can be very useful to keep on hand. Jars of peppers, sun-dried tomatoes and artichokes in olive oil make very good toppings, and will keep for quite a while in your larder.

The dough base

Although making your own base can be a little time-consuming, the method is very straightforward, and you end up with a delicious home-baked dish, as well as a sense of achievement. The ingredients are very basic:

YEAST There are three types of yeast available: fresh, dried and easy-blend. Fresh is usually found in health-food shops and is not expensive. Buy it in bulk and freeze in 15 g/½ oz quantities ready to use whenever needed.

Dissolve 15 g/½ oz fresh yeast in 90 ml/3½ fl oz tepid water with 2.5 ml/½ tsp sugar and allow it to froth before adding it to the flour – about 5 minutes. The frothiness indicates that the yeast is working. Fresh yeast will keep for 4–5 days in the refrigerator. Make sure it is well covered, as it will dry out very quickly.

Dried yeast is sold in sachets or drums by most supermarkets and chemists. It has a shelf-life of about six months, so buy only a small drum if you are not going to make bread dough on a regular basis. Like fresh yeast, add it to the tepid water with a little sugar, and stir to dissolve. Allow the mixture to stand for 10–15 minutes until froth develops on the surface.

Easy-blend yeast is the simplest to use as it is simply stirred dry into the flour before the water is added. It is sold in sachets by most supermarkets.

FLOUR Traditional pizza bases are made from bread dough, which is usually made with strong plain bread flour. You could also use one of the many types of wholemeal (whole wheat) flours available, such as stoneground wholemeal (whole wheat), wheatmeal and granary. Try adding a handful of wheatgerm or bran to white flour for extra flavour, fibre and interest. Or you could mix equal quantities of wholemeal (whole wheat) and white flour.

Always sift the flour first, as this will remove any lumps and help to incorporate air in the flour, which will in turn help to produce a light dough. If you sift wholemeal (whole wheat) flours, there will be some bran and other bits left in the sieve, which are normally tipped back so that their goodness and fibre are added to the sifted flour.

Yeast thrives in warm surroundings, so all the ingredients and equipment for the dough should be warm. If tepid yeast liquid is added to a cold bowl containing cold flour, it will quickly cool down. This will retard the growth of the yeast, and the dough will take much longer to rise. If the flour is kept in a cool cupboard or larder, remember to get it out in enough time for it to warm to room temperature before you use it. Sift the flour into a large mixing bowl, then place it somewhere warm, such as an airing cupboard or in the oven on the lowest setting. Do not allow it to overheat, as this will kill the yeast.

SALT Add the required amount of salt to the flour when sifting, as this will help to distribute it evenly throughout the resulting mixture. Salt is important, as it helps to develop the gluten in the flour. Gluten is the protein which produces the characteristic elasticity of the dough, but mostly it provides the dough with its flavour.

WATER It has been said that Naples produces the best pizzas because of the quality of its water! But as that may be a bit far to travel just to make a pizza, your local water will have to suffice. The water must be tepid, as this is the optimum temperature for the yeast to grow. Take care to add just the right amount of water stated in the recipe. If you add too much water, the dough will be difficult to handle and the cooked base will be too hard.

OIL For the best flavour always use a good quality olive oil, such as extra virgin.

Kneading the dough

This can be the most daunting procedure but it is a very necessary one. The kneading process mixes all the ingredients together and strengthens the gluten, which holds the bubbles of air created by the yeast, which in turn causes the dough to rise. The best way of doing it is to take the edge of the dough that is furthest away from you and pull it into the centre towards you, then push it down with the heel of your hand, turning the dough round with your other hand as you go. The dough must be kneaded for at least 10 minutes or until it becomes very smooth and pliable and is no longer sticky. If time is short, knead the dough in a food processor for a few minutes.

Place the dough in an oiled bowl, turning once so the surface is coated. Cover with clingfilm (plastic wrap) and leave to rise in a warm place for 1–2 hours until doubled in size.

Bread dough bases can be kept for several days before being used. After kneading, carefully wrap in clingfilm (plastic wrap) to prevent them from drying out in the refrigerator. Allow extra time for the dough to rise, as it will take a while for the dough to warm up and for the yeast to begin to work.

Toppings

There are a number of classic ingredients that are used regularly in pizza toppings. These include tomato sauce, olives, anchovies, capers, mushrooms, (bell) peppers, artichokes and chillies, as well as cheese and herbs. Be adventurous and experiment, but don't be afraid to stick to simple combinations of just two or three ingredients. The simplest pizzas are often the most delicious and memorable as the flavours don't fight each other.

When making pizza for several people with differing tastes, place different toppings on separate sections of the pizza, or make individual ones in a selection of flavours. They can all cook at the same time, making it easy to suit all tastes.

TOMATO SAUCE Most pizzas have tomato sauce as the basis for the topping. This can be made using either canned or fresh tomatoes. There are many types of canned tomato available – for example, whole plum tomatoes, chopped tomatoes, or chopped sieved tomato (passata). Canned chopped tomatoes may have added ingredients such as garlic, basil, onion, chilli and mixed herbs, which will add more interest to the sauce. Make sure the sauce is well seasoned before spreading it on the base, as a tasteless sauce will spoil your pizza.

The sauce will keep well in a screw-topped jar in the refrigerator for up to a week, or can be frozen if you need to keep it for longer periods.

CHEESE The cheese most often associated with the pizza is, of course, Mozzarella. It is a mild, white, delicate cheese traditionally made from buffalo milk. The best feature of this cheese as far as pizzas are concerned is its ability to melt and produce strings of cheese when a slice is cut and pulled away. It is sold in supermarkets, wrapped in small bags of whey to keep it moist. Slice, grate or cut it into small pieces before placing it on the pizza. Many supermarkets stock bags of pre-grated Mozzarella cheese, which is a great timesaver.

The other cheeses most often found on pizzas are Parmesan and Cheddar. If you are using strongly flavoured topping ingredients such as anchovies and olives, a milder-tasting cheese may be more suitable. Experiment with different cheeses to suit your taste.

HERBS Whenever possible, use fresh herbs. They are readily available, especially since the introduction of 'growing' herbs – small pots of herbs which you buy from the supermarket or greengrocer and grow at home. This not only ensures the herbs are as fresh as possible, but also provides a continuous supply.

If you use dried herbs, remember that you need only about one third of dried to fresh. The most popular pizza herbs are basil, oregano and parsley, although you can experiment with your favourite ones. Torn leaves of fresh basil on a tomato base is a simple but deliciously aromatic combination.

Successful baking

The secret of a crisp, chewy base is to bake pizzas at a very high temperature for as short a time as possible. Traditionally, pizzas are cooked in special ovens on a stone hearth. A large peel or paddle is used to slide them in and out. Baking on a pizza stone produces the best results at home. Alternatively, use a baking sheet (cookie sheet) or a perforated pizza pan – the holes allow heat and air to reach the centre of the base, resulting in a crisp, evenly cooked crust. Grease the pizza pan or baking sheet (cookie sheet) well, to prevent the pizza from sticking.

Always push up the edge of the dough to form a rim to prevent the topping from spilling over while it cooks.

Serving

Pizzas should be served as soon as they leave the oven as the cheese will set slightly and lose its elasticity as it cools down. Use a couple of large fish slices to transfer the pizza to the serving plate. Always use a warmed serving plate to prevent the pizza from going cold too quickly.

Cut the pizza into wedges or strips using a sharp knife or pizza cutter. As pizza slices are easy to eat by hand, they make great party food.

Crisp salads, coleslaw and garlic bread are ideal accompaniments and help to make a balanced meal. Because of their rich flavour pizzas are best served with Italian table wine such Valpolicella, Chianti or a well-chilled Frascati. If you are not a wine drinker, beer will go with pizza just as well.

Follow a pizza meal with a refreshing dessert, such as fresh fruit salad, sorbet or ice cream. Zabaglione, a light Italian dessert of eggs, sugar and Marsala wine, makes a perfect ending.

Freezing

Pizzas are ideal standby food, as you can make and freeze them in advance, and both the bread dough and the complete pizza can be frozen. Make up double quantities of dough and freeze the half that is unused after it has been kneaded. Wrap in clingfilm (plastic wrap) and place in a freezer bag. Defrost at room temperature and allow to rise as normal. Alternatively, rise and roll out the dough, top with tomato sauce, cheese and any other topping ingredients and bake for only 10 minutes. Cool, wrap in a polythene bag and place in the freezer. Cook straight from the freezer in a hot oven for about 15 minutes.

ANTIPASTI & ACCOMPANIMENTS

The word antipasto means 'before the main course' and what is served may be simple and inexpensive or highly elaborate. Antipasti usually come in three categories: meat, fish and vegetables. There are many varieties of cold meats, including ham, invariably sliced paper-thin. All varieties of fish are combined for the antipasto di pesce, including inkfish, octopus and cuttlefish. Huge prawns (shrimp), mussels and fresh sardines are always popular.

Numerous vegetables feature in Italian cuisine and are an important part of the daily diet. They are served as an antipasto, as an accompaniment to the meat or fish course, or occasionally as a course of their own. They are prepared in a variety of ways – raw or marinated, deep-fried or pickled, with and without dressings. Always cook vegetables only until 'al dente' and still slightly crisp. That way, they retain more nutrients and the colours remain bright, contrasting appealingly and deliciously with other parts of the meal.

Mediterranean (Bell) Pepper Salad

Colourful marinated Mediterranean vegetables make a tasty starter.
Serve with fresh bread or Tomato Toasts.

SERVES 4

INGREDIENTS

1 onion
2 red (bell) peppers
2 yellow (bell) peppers
3 tbsp olive oil
2 large courgettes (zucchini), sliced
2 garlic cloves, sliced
1 tbsp balsamic vinegar
50 g/1¾ oz anchovy fillets, chopped
30 g/1 oz/¼ cup black olives, halved and pitted
1 tbsp chopped fresh basil
salt and pepper

TOMATO TOASTS

small stick of French bread
1 garlic clove, crushed
1 tomato, peeled and chopped
2 tbsp olive oil
salt and pepper

1 Cut the onion into wedges. Core and deseed the (bell) peppers and cut into thick slices.

2 Heat the oil in a large heavy-based frying pan (skillet). Add the onion, (bell) peppers, courgettes (zucchini) and garlic, and fry gently for 20 minutes, stirring occasionally.

3 Add the vinegar, anchovies, olives and seasoning to taste, mix thoroughly and leave to cool.

4 Spoon on to individual plates and sprinkle with the basil.

5 To make the tomato toasts, cut the French bread diagonally into 1 cm/½ inch slices.

6 Mix the garlic, tomato, oil, and seasoning together, and spread thinly over each slice of bread.

7 Place on a baking sheet (cookie sheet), drizzle with the olive oil and bake in a preheated oven, 220°C/425°F/Gas Mark 7, for 5–10 minutes until crisp.

Step *1*

Step *2*

Step *3*

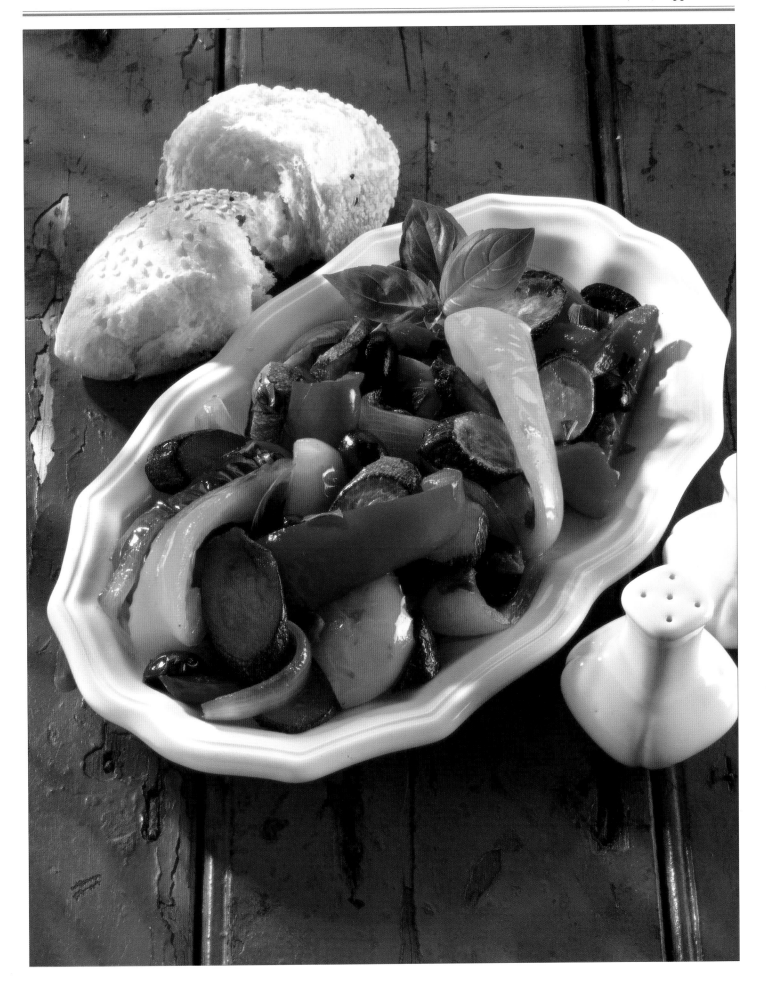

Preserved Meats (Salumi)

*Mix an attractive selection of these preserved meats (Salumi) with olives
and marinated vegetables for extra colour and variety.*

SERVES 4

INGREDIENTS

3 ripe tomatoes
3 ripe figs
1 small melon
60 g/2 oz Italian salami, sliced thinly
4 thin slices mortadella
6 slices Parma ham (prosciutto)
6 slices bresaola
4 fresh basil leaves, chopped
olive oil
90 g/3 oz/½ cup marinated olives, pitted
freshly ground black pepper, to serve

1 Slice the tomatoes thinly.

2 Cut the figs into quarters.

3 Halve the melon, scoop out the seeds, and cut the flesh into wedges.

4 Arrange the meats on one half of a serving platter. Arrange the tomato slices in the centre and sprinkle with the basil leaves and oil.

5 Cover the rest of the platter with the fruit and scatter the olives over the meats.

6 Serve with a little extra olive oil to drizzle over the bresaola, and coarsely ground black pepper.

Step *1*

Step *2*

Step *4*

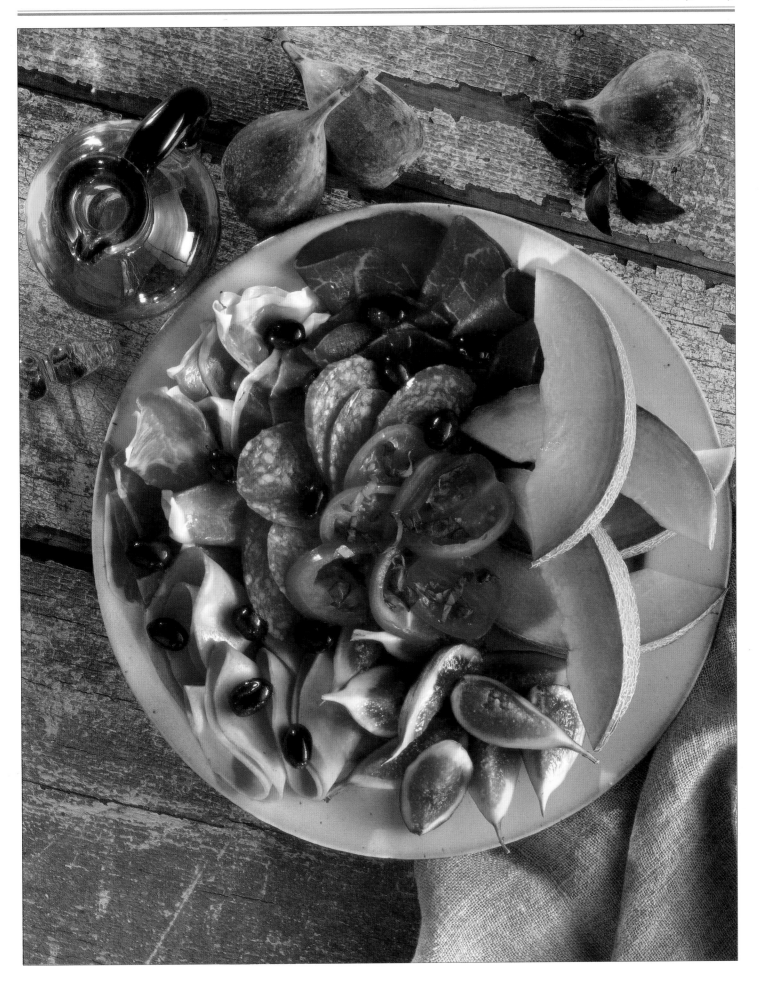

Mozzarella in Carozza

*A delicious way of serving Mozzarella – the cheese stretches out into
melted strings as you cut into the Carozza.*

SERVES 4

INGREDIENTS

200 g/7 oz Mozzarella
4 slices, Parma ham (prosciutto), about 90 g/3 oz
8 two-day old slices white bread,
crusts removed
butter for spreading
2–3 eggs
3 tbsp milk
vegetable oil for deep-frying
salt and pepper

TOMATO AND PEPPER SAUCE

1 onion, chopped
2 garlic cloves, crushed
3 tbsp olive oil
1 red (bell) pepper, cored, deseeded and chopped
425 g/14 oz can peeled tomatoes
2 tbsp tomato purée (paste)
3 tbsp water
1 tbsp lemon juice
salt and pepper
flat-leaf parsley, to garnish (optional)

1 First make the sauce: fry the onion and garlic in the oil until soft. Add the (bell) pepper and continue to cook for a few minutes. Add the tomatoes, tomato purée (paste), water, lemon juice and seasoning. Bring to the boil, cover and simmer for 10–15 minutes or until tender. Cool the sauce a little, then purée or liquidize until smooth and return to a clean pan.

2 Cut the Mozzarella into four slices as large as possible; if the cheese is a square piece cut into eight slices. Trim the Parma ham (prosciutto) slices to the same size as the cheese.

3 Lightly butter the bread and use the cheese and ham to make four sandwiches, pressing the edges firmly together. If liked, they may be cut in half at this stage. Cover with clingfilm (plastic wrap) and chill.

4 Lightly beat the eggs with the milk and seasoning in a shallow dish.

5 Carefully dip the sandwiches in the egg mixture until well coated, and leave to soak for a few minutes if possible.

6 Heat the oil in a large pan or deep-frier until it just begins to smoke, or until a cube of bread browns in about 30 seconds. Fry the sandwiches in batches until golden brown on both sides. Drain well on crumpled paper towels and keep warm. Serve the sandwiches hot, with the reheated tomato and pepper sauce, and garnished with parsley.

Step *3*

Step *5*

Step *6*

Black Olive Pâté

*This pâté is delicious served as a starter on crisp tomato bread. It can also
be served as a cocktail snack on small rounds of fried bread.*

SERVES 4

INGREDIENTS

250 g/8 oz/1½ cups pitted
juicy black olives
1 garlic clove, crushed
finely grated rind of 1 lemon
4 tbsp lemon juice
30 g/1 oz/½ cup fresh breadcrumbs
60 g/2 oz/¼ cup full fat soft cheese
salt and pepper
lemon wedges, to garnish

1 Roughly chop the olives and mix with all the other ingredients except the salt and pepper. Pound until smooth, or place in a food processor and work until fully blended. Season to taste with salt and freshly ground black pepper.

2 Store in a screw-top jar and chill for several hours before using – this allows the flavours to develop.

3 For a delicious cocktail snack, use a pastry cutter to cut out small rounds from a thickly sliced loaf.

4 Fry the bread rounds in a mixture of olive oil and butter until they are a light golden brown. Drain on paper towels.

5 Top each round with a little of the pâté, garnish with lemon wedges and serve immediately. This pâté will keep chilled in an airtight jar for up to 2 weeks.

Step *1*

Step *3*

Step *4*

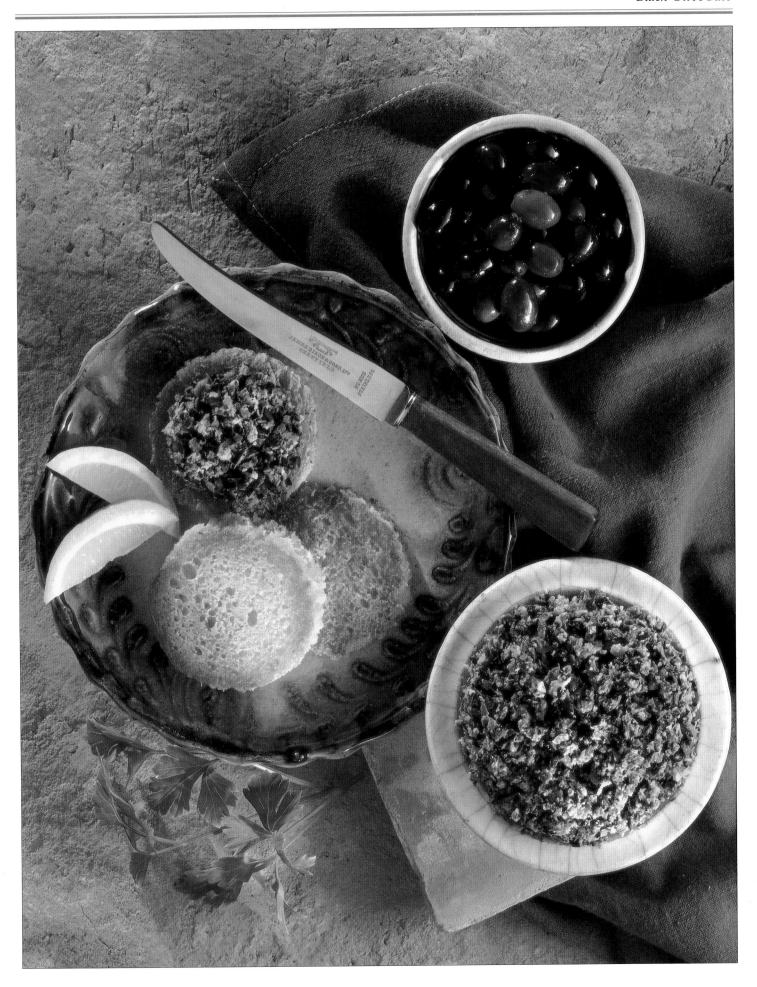

Roast (Bell) Pepper Salad

Serve chilled as an antipasto with cold meats, or warm as a side dish.
Garlic bread makes a delicious accompaniment.

SERVES 4

INGREDIENTS

4 large mixed red, green and yellow (bell) peppers
4 tbsp olive oil
1 large red onion, sliced
2 garlic cloves, crushed
4 tomatoes, peeled and chopped
pinch of sugar
1 tsp lemon juice
salt and pepper

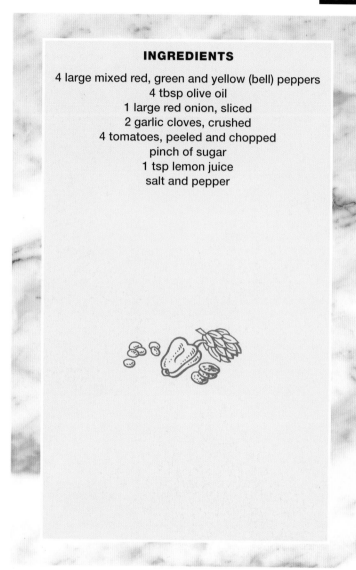

1 Trim and halve the (bell) peppers and remove the seeds.

2 Place the (bell) peppers skin-side up under a preheated hot grill (broiler). Cook until the skins char. Rinse under cold water and remove the skins.

3 Trim off any thick membranes and slice thinly.

4 Heat the oil and fry the onion and garlic until softened. Then add the (bell) peppers and tomatoes and fry over a low heat for 10 minutes.

5 Remove from the heat, add the sugar and lemon juice, and season to taste. Serve immediately or leave to cool. The flavours will continue to develop as the salad cools.

Step *2*

Step *3*

Step *4*

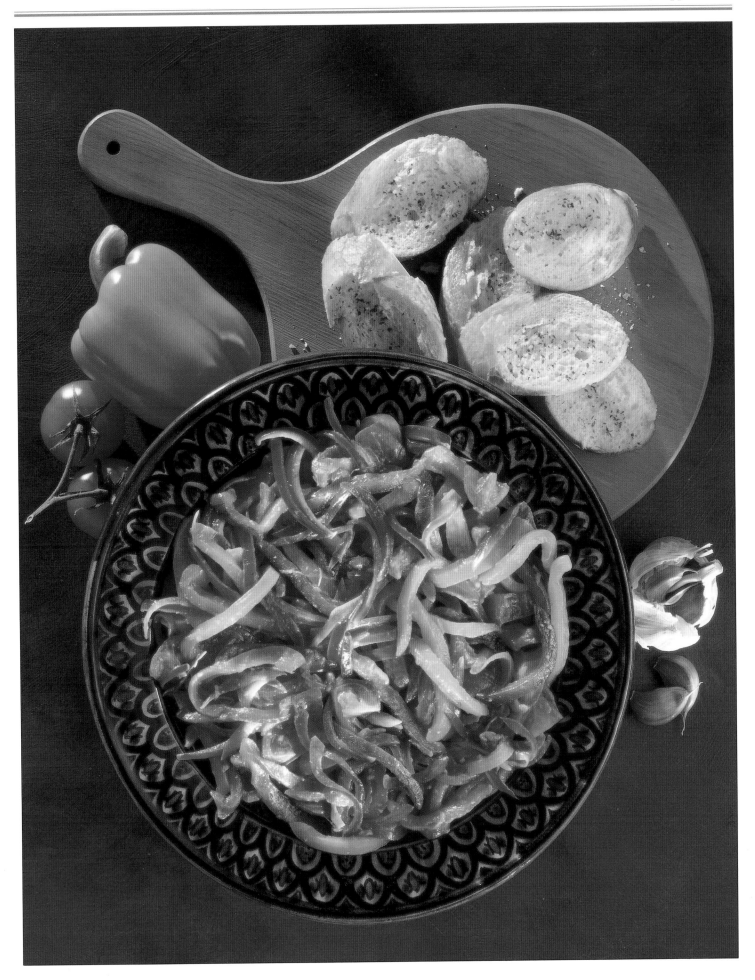

Seafood Salad

Seafood is plentiful in Italy and varieties of seafood salads are found everywhere. Each region has its own speciality.

SERVES 4

INGREDIENTS

175 g/6 oz squid rings, defrosted if frozen
600 ml/1 pint/2½ cups water
150 ml/¼ pint/⅔ cup dry white wine
250 g/8 oz hake or monkfish, cut into cubes
16–20 fresh mussels, scrubbed and
beards removed
20 clams in shells, scrubbed, if available
(otherwise use extra mussels)
125–175 g/4–6 oz peeled prawns (shrimp)
3–4 spring onions (scallions) trimmed
and sliced (optional)
radicchio and curly endive leaves, to serve
lemon wedges, to garnish

DRESSING

6 tbsp olive oil
1 tbsp wine vinegar
2 tbsp chopped fresh parsley
1–2 garlic cloves, crushed
salt and pepper

GARLIC MAYONNAISE

5 tbsp thick mayonnaise
2–3 tbsp fromage frais or natural yogurt
2 garlic cloves, crushed
1 tbsp capers
2 tbsp chopped fresh parsley or mixed herbs

1 Poach the squid in the water and wine for 20 minutes or until nearly tender. Add the fish and continue to cook gently for 7–8 minutes or until tender. Strain, reserving the fish. Pour the stock into a clean pan.

2 Bring the fish stock to the boil and add the mussels and clams. Cover the pan and simmer gently for about 5 minutes or until the shells open. Discard any that stay closed.

3 Drain the shellfish and remove from their shells. Put into a bowl with the cooked fish and add the prawns (shrimp) and onions (scallions) if using.

4 For the dressing, whisk together the oil, vinegar, parsley, garlic, salt and plenty of black pepper. Pour over the fish, mixing well. Cover and chill for several hours.

5 Arrange small leaves of radicchio and curly endive on four plates and spoon the fish salad into the centre. Garnish with lemon wedges. Combine all the ingredients for the garlic mayonnaise and serve with the salad.

Step *1*

Step *2*

Step *3*

Artichoke & Parma Ham (Prosciutto) Salad

Use bottled artichokes rather than canned ones, as they have a better flavour.

SERVES 4

INGREDIENTS

275 g/9 fl oz bottle artichokes in oil, drained
4 small tomatoes
30 g/1 oz/¼ cup sun-dried tomatoes,
cut into strips
30 g/1 oz/¼ cup black olives,
halved and pitted
30 g/1 oz/¼ cup Parma ham (prosciutto),
cut into strips
1 tbsp chopped fresh basil

FRENCH DRESSING

3 tbsp olive oil
1 tbsp wine vinegar
1 small garlic clove, crushed
½ tsp Dijon or Meaux mustard
1 tsp clear honey
salt and pepper

1 Drain the artichokes thoroughly, then cut them into quarters and place in a bowl.

2 Cut each tomato into six wedges and place in the bowl with the sun-dried tomatoes, olives and Parma ham (prosciutto).

3 To make the dressing, put all the ingredients into a screw-top jar and shake vigorously until the ingredients are thoroughly blended.

4 Pour the dressing over the salad and toss well together.

5 Transfer to individual plates and sprinkle with the basil.

Step *1*

Step *2*

Step *4*

Crostini alla Fiorentina

*Serve as a starter, or simply spread on small pieces of crusty fried bread
(crostini) as an appetizer with drinks.*

SERVES 4

INGREDIENTS

3 tbsp olive oil
1 onion, chopped
1 celery stalk, chopped
1 carrot, chopped
1–2 garlic cloves, crushed
125 g/4 oz chicken livers
125 g/4 oz calf's, lamb's or pig's liver
150 ml/¼ pint/⅔ cup red wine
1 tbsp tomato purée (paste)
2 tbsp chopped fresh parsley
3–4 canned anchovy fillets, chopped finely
2 tbsp stock or water
30–45 g/1–1½ oz/2–3 tbsp butter
1 tbsp capers
salt and pepper
small pieces of fried crusty bread, to serve
chopped parsley, to garnish

1 Heat the oil in a pan, add the onion, celery, carrot and garlic, and cook gently for 4–5 minutes or until the onion is soft, but not coloured.

2 Meanwhile, rinse and dry the chicken livers. Dry the calf's or other liver, and slice into strips. Add the liver to the pan and fry gently for a few minutes until the strips are well sealed on all sides.

3 Add half the wine and cook until mostly evaporated. Then add the rest of the wine, tomato purée (paste), half the parsley, the anchovy fillets, stock or water, a little salt and plenty of black pepper.

4 Cover the pan and simmer for 15–20 minutes or until tender and most of the liquid has been absorbed.

5 Cool the mixture a little, then either coarsely mince or put into a food processor and process to a chunky purée.

6 Return to the pan and add the butter, capers and remaining parsley. Heat through gently until the butter melts. Adjust the seasoning and turn into a bowl. Serve warm or cold spread on the slices of crusty bread and sprinkled with chopped parsley.

Step *2*

Step *3*

Step *6*

Tuna, Bean & Anchovy Salad

*Serve as part of a selection of antipasti, or for a summer lunch
with hot garlic bread.*

SERVES 4

INGREDIENTS

500 g/1 lb tomatoes
200 g/7 oz can tuna fish, drained
2 tbsp chopped fresh parsley
½ cucumber
1 small red onion, sliced
250 g/8 oz cooked French (green) beans,
1 small red (bell) pepper, cored and deseeded
1 small crisp lettuce
6 tbsp French dressing
3 hard-boiled (hard-cooked) eggs
60 g/2 oz can anchovies, drained
12 black olives, pitted

1 Cut the tomatoes into wedges, flake the tuna fish and put both into the bowl with the parsley.

2 Cut the cucumber in half lengthways, then cut into slices. Slice the onion. Add the cucumber and onion to the bowl.

3 Cut the French (green) beans in half, chop the red (bell) pepper and add both to the bowl with the lettuce leaves.

4 Pour over the French dressing and toss thoroughly, then spoon into a salad bowl to serve.

5 Cut the eggs into quarters, arrange over the top with the anchovies and scatter with the olives.

Step *1*

Step *2*

Step *3*

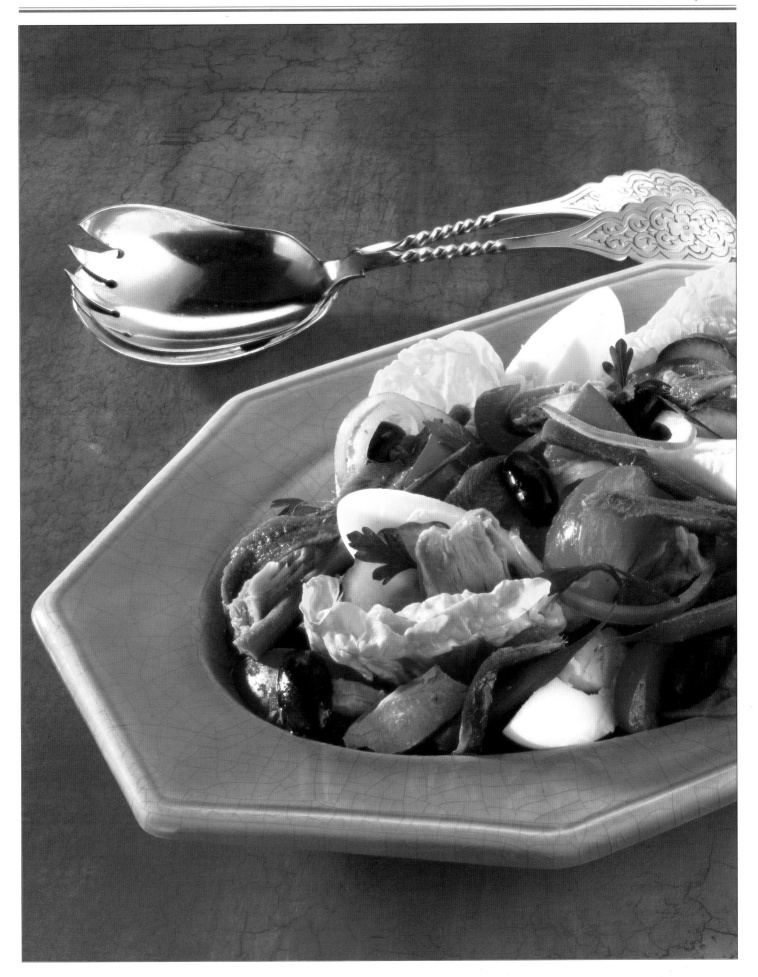

Warm Pasta with Basil Vinaigrette

*Sun-dried tomatoes and olives enhance this delicious pesto-inspired
salad, which is just as tasty served cold.*

SERVES 4–6

INGREDIENTS

250 g/8 oz pasta spirals
4 tomatoes, peeled
60 g/2 oz/½ cup black olives
30 g/1 oz/¼ cup sun-dried tomatoes
2 tbsp pine kernels (nuts), toasted
2 tbsp Parmesan shavings
sprig of fresh basil, to garnish

BASIL VINAIGRETTE

4 tbsp chopped fresh basil
1 garlic clove, crushed
2 tbsp freshly grated Parmesan
4 tbsp olive oil
2 tbsp lemon juice
pepper

1 Cook the pasta in boiling salted water for 10–12 minutes until al dente. Drain and rinse well in hot water, then drain again thoroughly.

2 To make the vinaigrette, whisk the basil, garlic, Parmesan, olive oil, lemon juice and pepper until well blended.

3 Put the pasta into a bowl, pour over the basil vinaigrette and toss thoroughly.

4 Cut the tomatoes into wedges. Halve and pit the olives and slice the sun-dried tomatoes.

5 Add the tomatoes, olives and sun-dried tomatoes to the pasta and mix thoroughly. Transfer to a salad bowl and scatter the nuts and Parmesan shavings over the top. Serve warm, garnished with a sprig of basil.

Step *3*

Step *4*

Step *5*

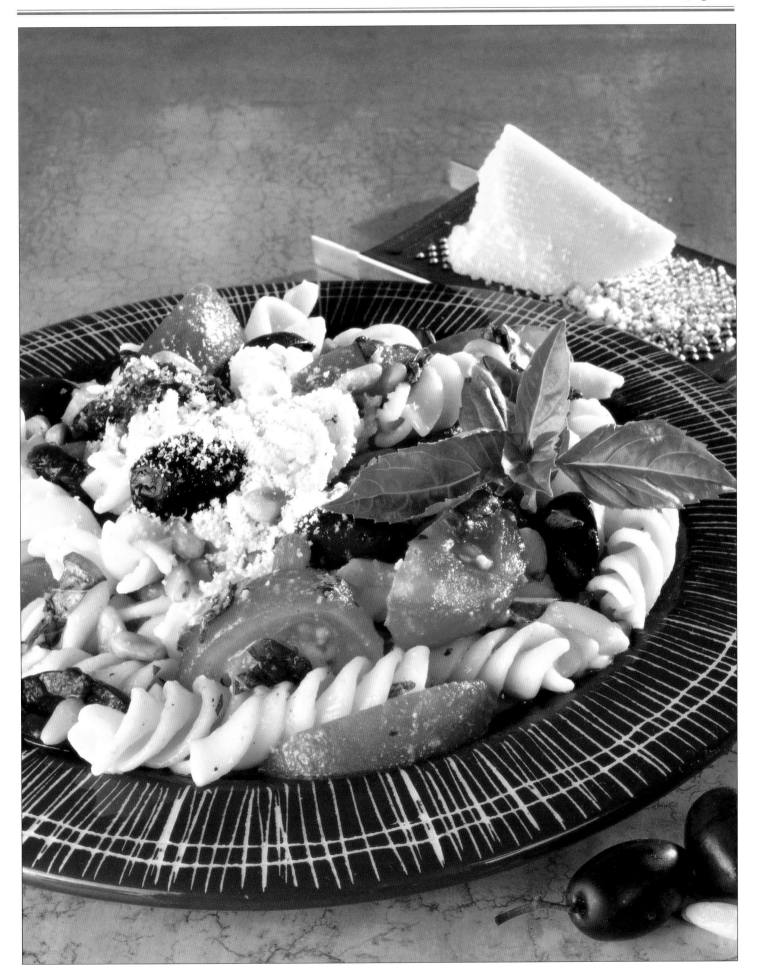

Aubergine (Eggplant) Salad

A starter with a difference from Sicily. It has a real bite, both from the sweet-sour sauce, and from the texture of the celery.

SERVES 4

INGREDIENTS

2 large aubergines (eggplant), about 1 kg/2 lb
6 tbsp olive oil
1 small onion, chopped finely
2 garlic cloves, crushed
6–8 celery stalks, cut into 1cm/½ inch slices
2 tbsp capers
12–16 green olives, pitted and sliced
2 tbsp pine kernels (nuts)
30 g/1 oz bitter or plain chocolate, grated
4 tbsp wine vinegar
1 tbsp brown sugar
salt and pepper
2 hard-boiled (hard-cooked) eggs, sliced, to serve
celery leaves or curly endive, to garnish

1 Cut the aubergines (eggplant) into 2.5 cm/1 inch cubes and sprinkle liberally with 2–3 tablespoons of salt. Leave to stand for an hour to extract the bitter juices, then rinse off the salt thoroughly under cold water, drain and dry on paper towels.

2 Heat most of the oil in a frying pan and fry the aubergines (eggplant) cubes until golden brown all over. Drain on paper towels then put in a large bowl.

3 Add the onion and garlic to the pan with the remaining oil and fry very gently until just soft. Add the celery to the pan and fry for a few minutes, stirring frequently, until lightly coloured but still crisp.

4 Add the celery to the aubergines (eggplant) with the capers, olives and pine kernels (nuts) and mix lightly.

5 Add the chocolate, vinegar and sugar to the residue in the pan. Heat gently until melted, then bring to the boil. Season with a little salt and plenty of freshly ground black pepper. Pour over the salad and mix lightly. Cover, leave until cold and then chill thoroughly.

6 Serve with sliced hard-boiled (hard-cooked) eggs and garnish with celery leaves or curly endive.

Step *2*

Step *4*

Step *5*

Baked Fennel Gratinati

*Fennel is often used in Italian cooking. In this dish its distinctive flavour
is offset by the smooth besciamella.*

SERVES 4

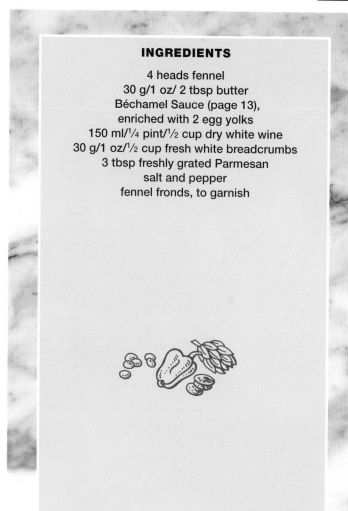

INGREDIENTS

4 heads fennel
30 g/1 oz/ 2 tbsp butter
Béchamel Sauce (page 13),
enriched with 2 egg yolks
150 ml/¼ pint/½ cup dry white wine
30 g/1 oz/½ cup fresh white breadcrumbs
3 tbsp freshly grated Parmesan
salt and pepper
fennel fronds, to garnish

1 Remove any bruised or tough outer stalks of fennel and cut each head in half.

2 Put into a saucepan of boiling salted water and simmer for 20 minutes until tender then drain.

3 Butter an ovenproof dish liberally and arrange the drained fennel in it.

4 Mix the wine into the white sauce and season to taste. Pour over the fennel.

5 Sprinkle evenly with the breadcrumbs and then the Parmesan.

6 Place in a preheated oven, 200°C/400°F/Gas Mark 6, and bake for 20 minutes until the top is golden. Serve garnished with fennel fronds.

Step *1*

Step *4*

Step *5*

Baked Aubergine (Eggplant) Parma-Style

Simmer the tomato sauce gently to reduce it slightly before using.

SERVES 4

INGREDIENTS

4 aubergines (eggplants), trimmed
3 tbsp olive oil
2 × 150g/5 oz packets Mozzarella, thinly sliced
4 slices Parma ham (prosciutto), shredded
1 tbsp chopped fresh marjoram
1 tbsp chopped fresh basil
½ quantity Béchamel Sauce (page 13)
30 g/1 oz/¼ cup Parmesan, grated
salt and pepper

TOMATO SAUCE

4 tbsp olive oil
1 large onion, sliced
4 garlic cloves, crushed
425 g/14 oz can chopped tomatoes
500 g/1lb fresh tomatoes, peeled and chopped
4 tbsp chopped fresh parsley
600 ml/1 pint/2½ cups hot vegetable stock
1 tbsp sugar
2 tbsp lemon juice
150 ml/¼ pint/⅔ cup dry white wine
salt and pepper

1 To make the sauce, heat the oil in a large saucepan. Fry the onion and garlic until beginning to soften. Add the canned and fresh tomatoes, parsley, stock, sugar and lemon juice. Cover and simmer for 15 minutes. Stir in the wine and season to taste.

2 Slice the aubergines (eggplant) thinly lengthways. Bring a large saucepan of water to the boil and cook the aubergine (eggplant) slices for 5 minutes.

3 Drain the aubergine (eggplant) slices on paper towels and pat dry.

4 Pour half the fresh tomato sauce into a greased ovenproof dish. Cover with half the cooked aubergines (eggplants) and drizzle with a little oil. Cover with half the Mozzarella, Parma ham (prosciutto) and herbs. Season to taste.

5 Repeat the layers and cover with the white sauce. Sprinkle with the Parmesan. Bake in a preheated oven, 190°C/375°F/Gas Mark 5, for 35–40 minutes until golden on top.

Step *2*

Step *3*

Step *4*

SOUPS

Soups are a very important part of the Italian cuisine.
They vary in consistency from light and delicate to
hearty main meal soups which need to be eaten with a
knife and fork. Texture is always apparent – Italians
rarely serve smooth soups. Some may be partially puréed
but the identity of the ingredients is never entirely
obliterated. There are regional characteristics too. In the
north, soups are often based on rice, while in Tuscany,
thick bean or bread-based soups are popular. Tomato,
garlic and pasta soups are typical of the south.
Minestrone is known world-wide but the best-known
version probably comes from Milan. However, all
varieties are full of vegetables and are delicious
and satisfying.

Fish soups abound in one guise or another, and most
of these are village specialities, so the variety is
unlimited. Many of these soups constitute a whole meal,
particularly those containing a large proportion of beans,
or with lightly toasted slices of bread added to the
bowl. For Italians, the time of year is important in
determining which soup will be served – vegetables,
roots, pulses (legumes) and herbs are always chosen
when they are in season and at the peak of perfection.

Minestrone with Pesto

One of the many versions of minestrone, which always contains a variety of vegetables, pasta and rice and often includes beans.

SERVES 6

INGREDIENTS

175 g/6 oz/scant 1 cup dried cannellini
beans, soaked overnight
2.5 litres/4 pints/10 cups water or stock
1 large onion, chopped
1 leek, trimmed and sliced thinly
2 celery stalks, sliced very thinly
2 carrots, chopped
3 tbsp olive oil
2 tomatoes, peeled and chopped roughly
1 courgette (zucchini), trimmed and sliced thinly
2 potatoes, diced
90 g/3 oz elbow macaroni
(or other small macaroni)
salt and pepper
4–6 tbsp freshly grated Parmesan

PESTO

2 tbsp pine kernels (nuts)
5 tbsp olive oil
2 bunches basil, stems removed
4–6 garlic cloves, crushed
90 g /3 oz/¹⁄₂ cup Pecorino or Parmesan, grated
salt and pepper

1 Drain the beans, rinse and put in a saucepan with the water or stock. Bring to the boil, cover and simmer gently for 1 hour.

2 Add the onion, leek, celery, carrots and oil. Cover and simmer for 4–5 minutes.

3 Add the tomatoes, courgette (zucchini), potatoes and macaroni and seasoning. Cover again and continue to simmer for about 30 minutes or until very tender.

4 Meanwhile, make the pesto. Fry the pine kernels (nuts) in 1 tablespoon of the oil until pale brown, then drain. Put the basil into a food processor or blender with the nuts and garlic. Process until well chopped. Alternatively, chop finely by hand and pound with a pestle and mortar. Gradually add the oil until smooth. Turn into a bowl, add the cheese and seasoning, and mix thoroughly.

5 Stir 1½ tablespoons of the pesto into the soup until well blended. Simmer for a further 5 minutes and adjust the seasoning. Serve very hot, sprinkled with the cheese.

Step *2*

Step *3*

Step *5*

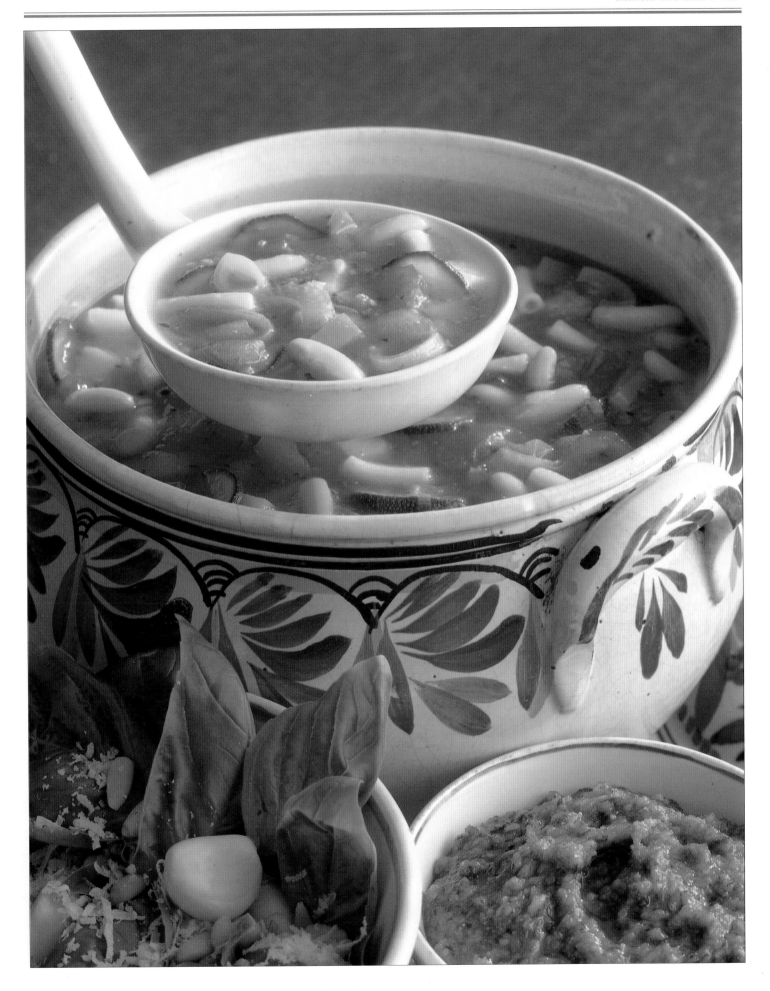

Red Bean Soup

Beans feature widely in Italian soups, making them hearty and tasty. You can use other varieties of beans in this soup, if preferred.

SERVES 4–6

INGREDIENTS

175 g/6 oz/scant 1 cup dried red kidney beans,
soaked overnight
1.7 litres/3 pints/7½ cups water
1 large ham bone or bacon knuckle
2 carrots, chopped
1 large onion, chopped
2 celery stalks, sliced thinly
1 leek, trimmed, washed and sliced
1–2 bay leaves
2 tbsp olive oil
2–3 tomatoes, peeled and chopped
1 garlic clove, crushed
1 tbsp tomato purée (paste)
60 g/2 oz/4 tbsp arborio or Italian rice
125–175 g/4–6 oz green cabbage, shredded finely
salt and pepper

1 Drain the beans and put into a saucepan with enough water to cover. Bring to the boil and boil hard for 15 minutes to remove any harmful toxins. Reduce the heat and simmer for 45 minutes.

2 Drain the beans and put into a clean saucepan with the water, ham bone or knuckle, carrots, onion, celery, leek, bay leaves and olive oil. Bring to the boil, then cover and simmer for an hour or until the beans are very tender.

3 Discard the bay leaves and bone, reserving any ham pieces from the bone. Remove a small cupful of the beans and reserve. Purée or liquidize the soup in a food processor or blender, or push through a coarse sieve (strainer), and return to a clean pan.

4 Add the tomatoes, garlic, tomato purée (paste), rice and plenty of seasoning. Bring back to the boil and simmer for about 15 minutes or until the rice is tender.

5 Add the cabbage and reserved beans and ham, and continue to simmer for 5 minutes. Adjust the seasoning and serve very hot. If liked, a piece of toasted crusty bread may be put in the base of each soup bowl before ladling in the soup. If the soup is too thick, add a little boiling water or stock.

Step *2*

Step *4*

Step *5*

Cream of Artichoke Soup

*A creamy soup with the unique, subtle flavouring of Jerusalem artichokes
and a garnish of grated carrots for extra crunch.*

SERVES 4-6

INGREDIENTS

750 g/1½ lb Jerusalem artichokes
1 lemon, sliced thickly
60 g/2 oz/¼ cup butter or margarine
2 onions, chopped
1 garlic clove, crushed
1.25 litres/2¼ pints/5½ cups chicken or
vegetable stock
2 bay leaves
¼ tsp ground mace or ground nutmeg
1 tbsp lemon juice
150 ml/¼ pint/⅔ cup single (light) cream or
natural fromage frais
salt and pepper

TO GARNISH

coarsely grated carrot
chopped fresh parsley or coriander (cilantro)

1 Peel and slice the artichokes. Put into a bowl of water with the lemon slices.

2 Melt the butter or margarine in a large saucepan. Add the onions and garlic, and fry gently for 3–4 minutes until soft but not coloured.

3 Drain the artichokes and add to the pan. Mix well and cook gently for 2–3 minutes without allowing to colour.

4 Add the stock, seasoning, bay leaves, mace or nutmeg and lemon juice. Bring slowly to the boil, then cover and simmer gently for about 30 minutes until the vegetables are very tender.

5 Discard the bay leaves. Cool the soup slightly then press through a sieve (strainer) or blend in a food processor until smooth. If liked, a little of the soup may be only partially puréed and added to the rest of the puréed soup, to give extra texture.

6 Pour into a clean pan and bring to the boil. Adjust the seasoning and stir in the cream or fromage frais. Reheat gently without boiling. Garnish with grated carrot and chopped parsley or coriander (cilantro).

Step *1*

Step *3*

Step *5*

Haricot Bean & Pasta Soup

A dish with proud Mediterranean origins, this soup is a winter warmer, to be served with warm, crusty bread and, if you like, a slice of cheese.

SERVES 4

INGREDIENTS

250 g/8 oz/generous 1 cup dried haricot beans, soaked, drained and rinsed
4 tbsp olive oil
2 large onions, sliced
3 garlic cloves, chopped
425 g/14 oz can chopped tomatoes
1 tsp dried oregano
1 tsp tomato purée (paste)
900 ml/1½ pints/3½ cups water
90 g/3 oz small pasta shapes, such as fusilli or conchigliette
125 g/4 oz sun-dried tomatoes, drained and sliced thinly
1 tbsp chopped coriander (cilantro), or flat-leaf parsley
2 tbsp freshly grated Parmesan
salt and pepper

1 Put the soaked beans into a large pan, cover with cold water and bring them to the boil. Boil rapidly for 15 minutes to remove any harmful toxins. Drain the beans in a colander.

2 Heat the oil in a pan over a medium heat and fry the onions until they are just beginning to change colour. Stir in the garlic and cook for 1 further minute. Stir in the chopped tomatoes, oregano and the tomato purée and pour on the water. Add the beans, bring to the boil and cover the pan. Simmer for 45 minutes, or until the beans are almost tender.

3 Add the pasta, season the soup and stir in the sun-dried tomatoes. Return the soup to the boil, partly cover the pan and continue cooking for 10 minutes, or until the pasta is nearly tender.

4 Stir in the chopped coriander (cilantro) or parsley. Taste the soup and adjust the seasoning if necessary. Transfer to a warmed soup tureen to serve. Sprinkle with the cheese and serve hot.

Step *2*

Step *3*

Step *4*

Fish Soup

There are many varieties of fish soup in Italy, some including shellfish.
This one, from Tuscany, is more like a chowder.

SERVES 4–6

INGREDIENTS

1 kg/2 lb assorted prepared fish (including
mixed fish fillets, squid, etc)
2 onions, sliced thinly
2 celery stalks, sliced thinly
a few sprigs of parsley
2 bay leaves
150 ml/¼ pint/⅔ cup white wine
1 litre/1¾ pints/4 cups water
2 tbsp olive oil
1 garlic clove, crushed
1 carrot, chopped finely
425 g/14 oz can peeled tomatoes, puréed
2 potatoes, chopped
1 tbsp tomato purée (paste)
1 tsp chopped fresh oregano or ½ tsp
dried oregano
350 g/12 oz fresh mussels
175 g/6 oz peeled prawns (shrimp)
2 tbsp chopped fresh parsley
salt and pepper
crusty bread, to serve

1 Cut the cleaned and prepared fish into slices or cubes and put into a large saucepan with half the onion and celery, the parsley sprigs, bay leaves, wine and water. Bring to the boil, then cover and simmer for about 25 minutes.

2 Strain the fish stock and discard the vegetables. Skin the fish, remove any bones and reserve.

3 Heat the oil in a pan, finely chop the remaining onion and fry with the garlic, carrot and remaining celery until soft but not coloured. Add the puréed canned tomatoes, potatoes, tomato purée (paste), oregano, reserved stock and seasonings. Bring to the boil and simmer for about 15 minutes or until the potato is almost tender.

4 Meanwhile, thoroughly scrub the mussels. Add to the pan with the prawns (shrimp) and simmer for about 5 minutes or until the mussels have opened (discard any that stay closed).

5 Return the fish to the soup with the chopped parsley, bring back to the boil and simmer for 5 minutes. Adjust the seasoning.

6 Serve the soup in warmed bowls with chunks of fresh crusty bread, or put a toasted slice of crusty bread in the bottom of each bowl before adding the soup. If possible, remove a few half shells from the mussels before serving.

Step *1*

Step *4*

Step *5*

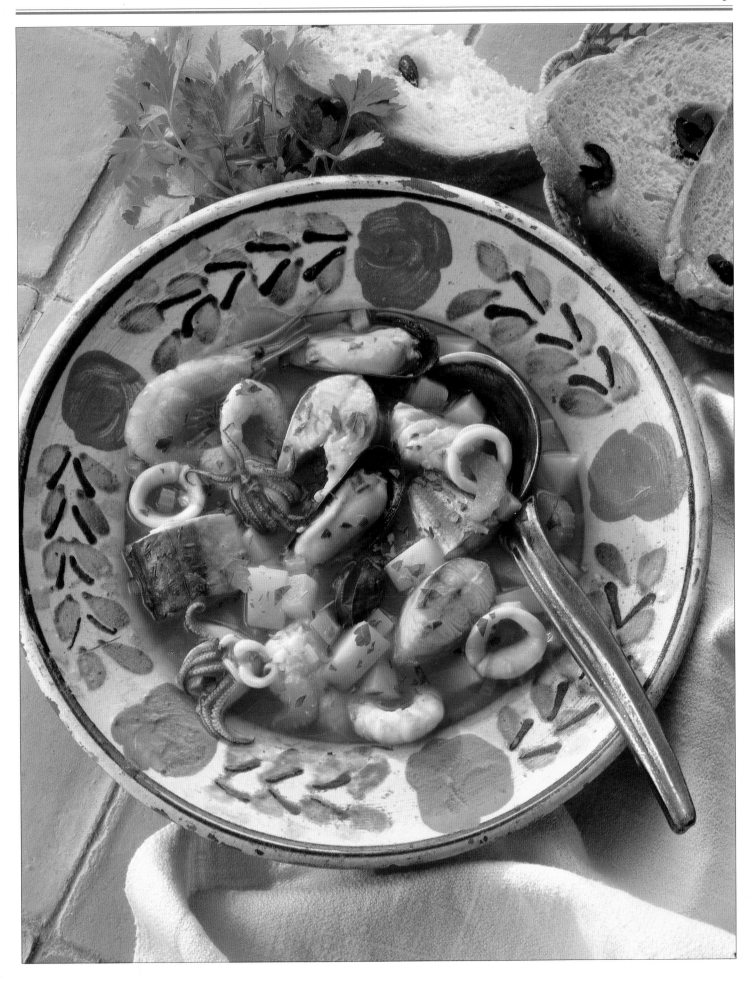

Mussels in White Wine

*This soup of mussels cooked in white wine with onions and cream, can be
served as an appetizer or a main dish, with plenty of crusty bread.*

SERVES 4

INGREDIENTS

about 3 litres/5 pints/12 cups fresh mussels
60 g/2 oz/¼ cup butter
1 large onion, chopped very finely
2–3 garlic cloves, crushed
350 ml/12 fl oz/1½ cups dry white wine
150 ml/¼ pint/⅔ cup water
2 tbsp lemon juice
good pinch of finely grated lemon rind
1 bouquet garni sachet
1 tbsp plain (all-purpose) flour
4 tbsp single (light) or double (thick) cream
2–3 tbsp chopped fresh parsley
salt and pepper
warm crusty bread, to serve

1 Scrub the mussels in several changes of cold water to remove all mud, sand, barnacles, etc. Pull off all the 'beards'. All the mussels must be tightly closed; if they don't close when given a sharp tap, they must be discarded.

2 Melt half the butter in a large saucepan. Add the onion and garlic, and fry gently until soft but not coloured.

3 Add the wine, water, lemon juice and rind, bouquet garni and plenty of seasoning. Bring to the boil then cover and simmer for 4–5 minutes.

4 Add the mussels to the pan, cover tightly and simmer for 5 minutes, shaking the pan frequently, until all the mussels have opened. Discard any mussels which have not opened. Remove the bouquet garni.

5 Remove the empty half shell from each mussel. Blend the remaining butter with the flour and whisk into the soup, a little at a time. Simmer gently for 2–3 minutes until slightly thickened.

6 Add the cream and half the parsley to the soup and reheat gently. Adjust the seasoning. Ladle the mussels and soup into warmed large soup bowls, sprinkle with the remaining parsley and serve with plenty of warm crusty bread.

Step *1*

Step *3*

Step *5*

PASTA DISHES

The simplicity and satisfying nature of pasta in all its varieties makes it a universal favourite. Easy to cook and easy on the purse, pasta is wonderfully versatile. It can be served in soups, with meat, fish or vegetable sauces, or baked in the oven.

Some of the most popular and best-known pasta dishes are ones that combine long strands of pasta cooked 'al dente', with a rich hearty meat sauce. Spaghetti Bolognese needs no introduction, and yet it is said that there are almost as many versions of this delicious regional dish as there are lovers of Italian food.

Fish and seafood are irresistible combined with pasta and need only the briefest of cooking times. Vermicelli with Clam Sauce, creamy Seafood Lasagne, and Pasta Shells with Mussels will all give you a whiff of the sea, if not the Mediterranean. Pasta combined with vegetables provides inspiration for countless dishes which will please vegetarians and meat-eaters alike.

Layered pasta dishes are perfect for parties, picnics, buffet meals or informal dinners. Children and teenagers love them. Try Aubergine Cake (page 76) or Layered Meatloaf (page 74). They will make popular additions to your repertoire of baked pasta favourites.

Spaghetti Carbonara

*Ensure all the cooked ingredients are as hot as possible, so that the beaten
eggs are cooked on contact. Serve this classic dish with a flourish.*

SERVES 4

INGREDIENTS

425 g/14 oz spaghetti
2 tbsp olive oil
1 large onion, sliced thinly
2 garlic cloves, chopped
175 g/6 oz streaky bacon rashers, rind
removed, cut into thin strips
30 g/1 oz/2 tbsp butter
175 g/6 oz mushrooms, sliced thinly
300 ml/½ pint/1¼ cups double (heavy) cream
3 eggs, beaten
90 g/3 oz/¾ cup Parmesan, grated, plus extra
to serve (optional)
freshly ground black pepper
sprigs of sage, to garnish

1 Heat a large serving dish or bowl. Cook the spaghetti
in a large pan of boiling salted water, adding
1 tablespoon of the oil. When the pasta is almost tender,
drain in a colander. Return the spaghetti to the pan, cover
and leave it in a warm place.

2 While the spaghetti is cooking, heat the remaining oil
in a frying pan (skillet) over a medium heat. Fry the
onion until it is translucent, then add the garlic and bacon
and fry until the bacon is crisp.

3 Remove the onion, garlic and bacon with a slotted
spoon and set aside to keep warm. Heat the butter in
the pan and fry the mushrooms for 3–4 minutes, stirring
them once or twice. Return the bacon mixture to the
mushrooms. Cover and keep warm.

4 Stir together the cream, the beaten eggs and cheese,
and season with salt and pepper.

5 Working very quickly to avoid cooling the cooked
ingredients, tip the spaghetti into the bacon and
mushroom mixture and pour on the eggs. Toss the
spaghetti quickly, using two forks, and serve it at once. If
you wish, serve with extra grated Parmesan.

Step *3*

Step *4*

Step *5*

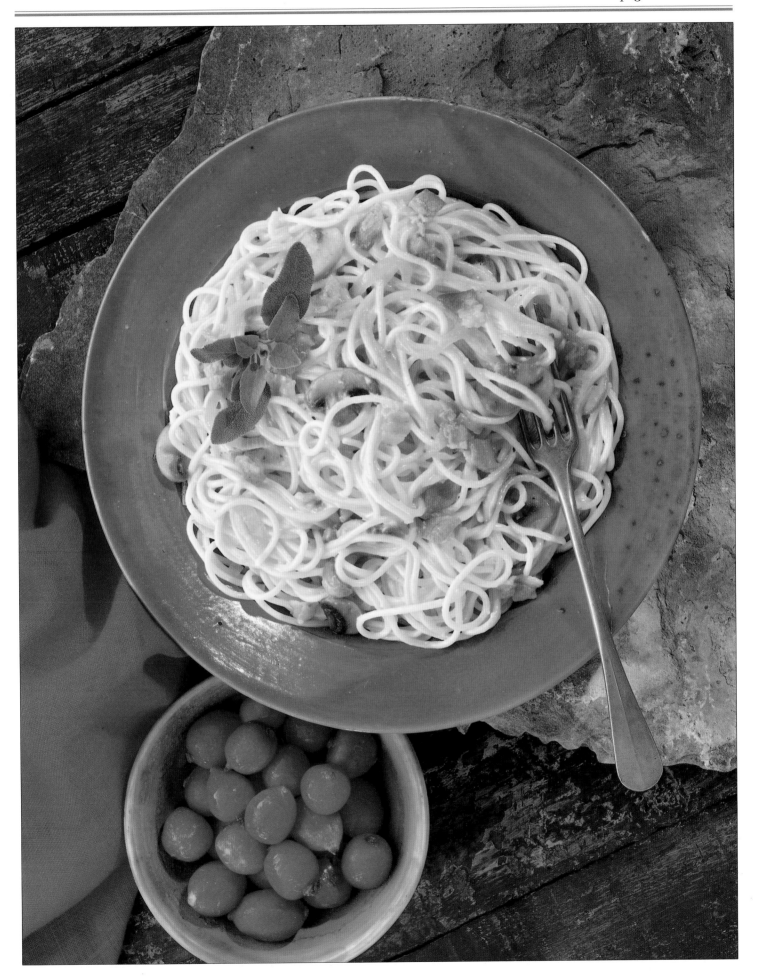

Tagliatelle with Chicken Sauce

*Spinach ribbon noodles covered with a rich tomato sauce and topped
with creamy chicken makes a very appetizing dish.*

SERVES 4

INGREDIENTS

Basic Tomato Sauce (page 13)
250 g/8 oz fresh green ribbon noodles
1 tbsp olive oil
salt
basil leaves, to garnish

CHICKEN SAUCE

60 g/2 oz/¼ cup unsalted butter
425 g/14 oz boned, skinned chicken breast,
thinly sliced
90 g/3 oz/¾ cup blanched almonds
300 ml/½ pint/1¼ cups double (heavy) cream
salt and pepper
basil leaves, to garnish

1 Make the tomato sauce, and keep warm.

2 To make the chicken sauce, melt the butter in a pan over a medium heat and fry the chicken strips and almonds for 5–6 minutes, stirring frequently, until the chicken is cooked through.

3 Meanwhile, pour the cream into a small pan over a low heat, bring it to the boil and boil for about 10 minutes, until reduced by almost half. Pour the cream over the chicken and almonds, stir well, and season. Set aside and keep warm.

4 Cook the pasta in a large pan of boiling salted water, first adding the oil. When the pasta is just tender, drain in a colander, then return it to the pan, cover and keep warm.

5 Turn the pasta into a warmed serving dish and spoon the tomato sauce over it. Spoon the chicken and cream over the centre, scatter the basil leaves over and serve at once.

Step *1*

Step *2*

Step *3*

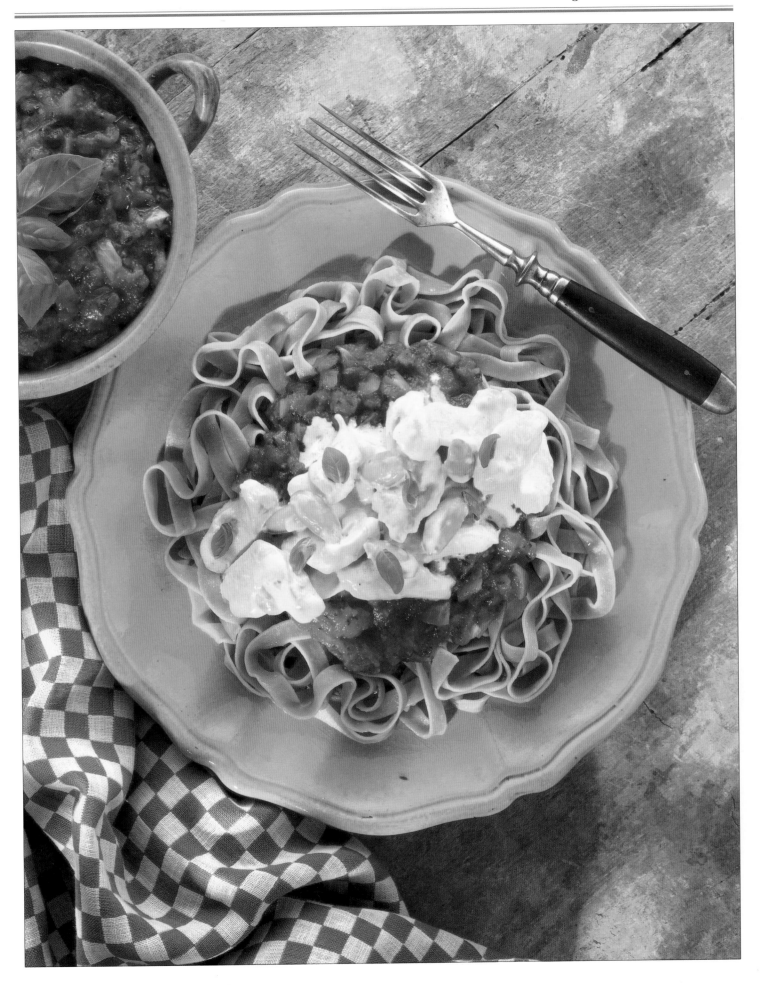

Spaghetti Bolognese

This familiar meat sauce, known as ragù, may also be used in lasagne, and in other baked dishes. It can be made in large quantities and frozen.

SERVES 4

INGREDIENTS

425 g/14 oz spaghetti
1 tbsp olive oil
salt
15 g/½ oz/1 tbsp butter
2 tbsp chopped fresh parsley, to garnish

RAGÙ

3 tbsp olive oil
45 g/1½ oz butter
2 large onions, chopped
4 celery stalks, sliced thinly
175 g/6 oz streaky bacon, chopped into small strips
2 garlic cloves, chopped
500 g/1 lb minced (ground) lean beef
2 tbsp tomato purée (paste)
1 tbsp flour
425 g/14 oz can chopped tomatoes
150 ml/¼ pint/⅔ cup beef stock
150 ml/¼ pint/⅔ cup red wine
2 tsp dried oregano
½ tsp freshly grated nutmeg
salt and pepper

1 To make the ragù: heat the oil and the butter in a large frying pan (skillet) over a medium heat. Add the onions, celery and bacon pieces and fry them together for 5 minutes, stirring once or twice.

2 Stir in the garlic and minced (ground) beef and cook, stirring, until the meat has lost its redness. Lower the heat and continue cooking for a further 10 minutes, stirring once or twice.

3 Increase the heat to medium, stir in the tomato purée (paste) and the flour and cook for 1–2 minutes. Stir in the chopped tomatoes, beef stock and wine, and bring to the boil, stirring. Season the sauce and stir in the oregano and nutmeg. Cover the pan and simmer for 45 minutes, stirring occasionally.

4 Cook the spaghetti in a large pan of boiling salted water, adding the olive oil. When it is almost tender, drain in a colander, then return to the pan. Dot the spaghetti with the butter and toss thoroughly.

5 Taste the sauce and adjust the seasoning if necessary. Pour the sauce over the spaghetti and toss well. Sprinkle with the parsley and serve immediately.

Step *1*

Step *2*

Step *3*

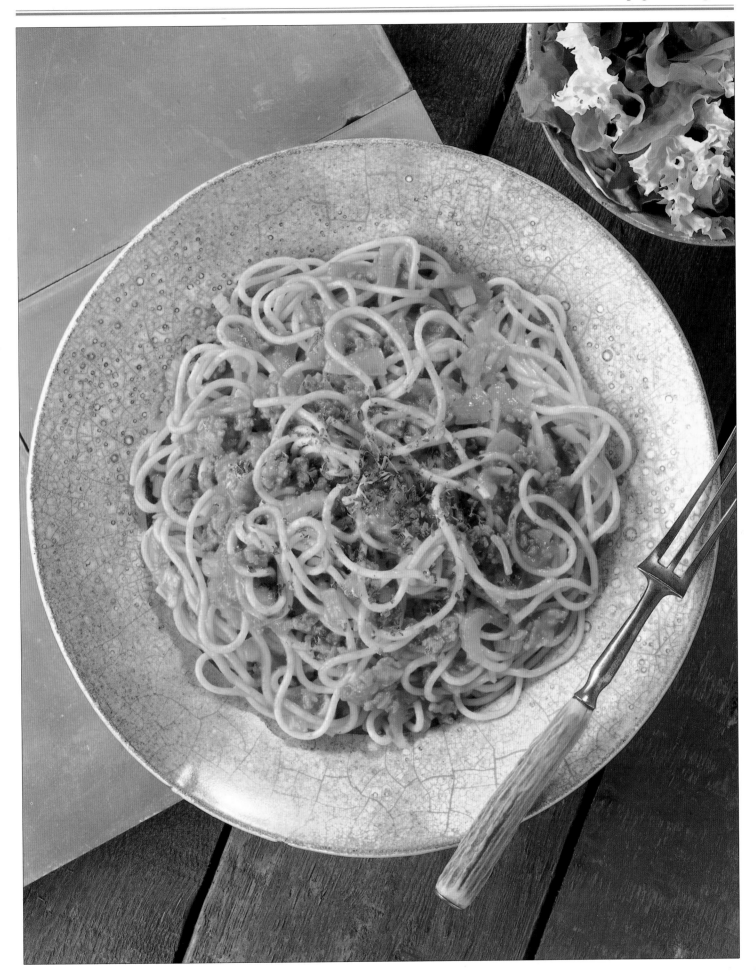

Tagliatelle with Meatballs

*There is an appetizing contrast of textures and
flavours in this satisfying family dish.*

SERVES 4

INGREDIENTS

500 g/1 lb minced (ground) lean beef
60 g/2 oz/1 cup soft white breadcrumbs
1 garlic clove, crushed
2 tbsp chopped fresh parsley
1 tsp dried oregano
large pinch of freshly grated nutmeg
¼ tsp ground coriander
60 g/2 oz/½ cup Parmesan, grated
2–3 tbsp milk
flour, for dusting
4 tbsp olive oil
425 g/14 oz tagliatelli
30 g/1 oz/2 tbsp butter, diced
salt
2 tbsp chopped fresh parsley, to garnish

SAUCE

3 tbsp olive oil
2 large onions, sliced
2 celery stalks, sliced thinly
2 garlic cloves, chopped
425 g/14 oz can chopped tomatoes
125 g/4 oz bottled sun-dried tomatoes,
drained and chopped
2 tbsp tomato purée (paste)
1 tbsp dark muscovado sugar
150 ml/¼ pint/⅔ cup white wine, or water
salt and pepper
green salad, to serve

1 To make the sauce, heat the oil in a frying pan and fry the onion and celery until translucent. Add the garlic and cook for 1 minute. Stir in the tomatoes, tomato purée (paste), sugar and wine, and season. Bring to the boil and simmer for 10 minutes.

2 Break up the meat in a bowl with a wooden spoon until it becomes a sticky paste. Stir in the breadcrumbs, garlic, herbs and spices. Stir in the cheese and enough milk to make a firm paste. Flour your hands, take large spoonfuls of the mixture and shape it into twelve balls. Heat the oil in a frying pan and fry the meatballs for 5–6 minutes until browned.

3 Pour the tomato sauce over the meatballs. Lower the heat, cover the pan and simmer for 30 minutes, turning once or twice. Add a little extra water if the sauce begins to dry.

4 Cook the pasta in a large saucepan of boiling salted water, adding the remaining oil. When almost tender, drain in a colander, then turn into a warmed serving dish, dot with the butter and toss with two forks. Spoon the meatballs and sauce over the pasta and sprinkle on the parsley. Serve with a green salad.

Step *1*

Step *2*

Step *3*

Lasagne Verde

The sauce in this delicious baked pasta dish is the same sauce that is served with Spaghetti Bolognese (page 66).

SERVES 6

INGREDIENTS

Ragù (page 66)
1 tbsp olive oil
250 g/8 oz lasagne verde
60 g/2 oz/½ cup Parmesan, grated
Béchamel Sauce (page 13)
salt and pepper
green salad, tomato salad or
black olives, to serve

1 Begin by making the ragù as described on page 66. Cook for 10–12 minutes longer than the time given, in an uncovered pan, to allow the excess liquid to evaporate. To layer the sauce with lasagne, it needs to be reduced to the consistency of a thick paste.

2 Have ready a large pan of boiling, salted water and add the olive oil. Drop the pasta sheets into the boiling water a few at a time, and return the water to the boil before adding further pasta sheets. If you are using fresh lasagne, cook the sheets for a total of 8 minutes. If you are using dried or partly precooked pasta, cook it according to the directions given on the packet.

3 Remove the pasta sheets from the pan with a slotted spoon. Spread them in a single layer on damp tea towels (dish cloths).

4 Grease a rectangular ovenproof dish, about 25–28 cm/10–11 inches long. To assemble the dish, spoon a little of the meat sauce into the prepared dish, cover with a layer of lasagne, then spoon over a little béchamel sauce and sprinkle some of the cheese. Continue making layers in this way, covering the final layer of lasagne with the remaining béchamel sauce.

5 Sprinkle on the remaining cheese and bake in the preheated oven, 190°C/375°F/Gas Mark 5, for 40 minutes, until the sauce is golden brown and bubbling. Serve with a green salad, a tomato salad, or a bowl of black olives.

Step *2*

Step *3*

Step *4*

Stuffed Cannelloni

*Cannelloni, the thick round pasta tubes, make perfect containers
for close-textured sauces of all kinds.*

SERVES 4

INGREDIENTS

8 cannelloni tubes
1 tbsp olive oil
fresh herb sprigs, to garnish

FILLING

30 g/1 oz/2 tbsp butter
300 g/10 oz frozen spinach, defrosted
and chopped
125 g/4 oz /$\frac{1}{2}$ cup Ricotta
30 g/1 oz/$\frac{1}{4}$ cup Parmesan, grated
60 g/2 oz/$\frac{1}{4}$ cup chopped ham
$\frac{1}{4}$ tsp freshly grated nutmeg
2 tbsp double (heavy) cream
2 eggs, lightly beaten
salt and pepper

SAUCE

30 g/1 oz/2 tbsp butter
30 g/1 oz/$\frac{1}{4}$ cup flour
300 ml/$\frac{1}{2}$ pint/1$\frac{1}{4}$ cups milk
2 bay leaves
large pinch of grated nutmeg
30 g/1 oz /$\frac{1}{4}$ cup Parmesan, grated

1 To prepare the filling, melt the butter in a pan and stir in the spinach. Stir for 2–3 minutes to allow the moisture to evaporate, then remove the pan from the heat. Stir in the cheeses and the ham. Season with nutmeg, and salt and pepper. Beat in the cream and eggs to make a thick paste. Set aside to cool.

2 Cook the cannelloni in a large pan of boiling salted water, adding the olive oil. When almost tender, after 10–12 minutes, drain in a colander and set aside to cool.

3 To make the sauce, melt the butter in a pan, stir in the flour and, when it has formed a roux, gradually pour on the milk, stirring all the time. Add the bay leaves, bring to simmering point, and cook for 5 minutes. Season with nutmeg, salt and pepper. Remove the pan from the heat and discard the bay leaves.

4 To assemble the dish, spoon the filling into a piping bag and pipe it into each of the cannelloni tubes.

5 Spoon a little of the sauce into a shallow baking dish. Arrange the cannelloni in a single layer, then pour over the remaining sauce. Sprinkle on the remaining Parmesan cheese and bake in the preheated oven, 190°C/375°F/Gas Mark 5, for 40–45 minutes, until the sauce is golden brown and bubbling. Serve garnished with fresh herb sprigs.

Step *2*

Step *4*

Step *5*

Layered Meat Loaf

*The cheesy pasta layer comes as a pleasant surprise inside
this lightly spiced meat loaf.*

SERVES 6

INGREDIENTS

30 g/1 oz/2 tbsp butter, plus extra for greasing
1 onion, chopped finely
1 small red (bell) pepper, cored, deseeded
and chopped
1 garlic clove, chopped
500 g/1 lb minced (ground) lean beef
30 g/1 oz/½ cup soft white breadcrumbs
½ tsp cayenne pepper
1 tbsp lemon juice
½ tsp grated lemon rind
2 tbsp chopped fresh parsley
90 g/3 oz short pasta, such as fusilli
4 bay leaves
1 tbsp olive oil
Cheese Sauce (page 14)
175 g/6 oz streaky bacon rashers, rind removed
salt and pepper
salad leaves, to garnish

1 Melt the butter in a pan over a medium heat and fry the onion and pepper for about 3 minutes, until the onion is translucent. Stir in the garlic and cook for a further 1 minute.

2 Put the meat into a large bowl and mash it with a wooden spoon until it becomes a sticky paste. Tip in the fried vegetables and stir in the breadcrumbs, cayenne, lemon juice, lemon rind and parsley. Season the mixture with salt and pepper and set aside.

3 Cook the pasta in a large pan of boiling water to which you have added salt and the olive oil. When it is almost tender, drain in a colander. Stir the pasta into the cheese sauce.

4 Grease a 1 kg/2 lb loaf tin and arrange the bay leaves in the base. Stretch the bacon rashers with the back of a knife blade and arrange them to line the base and the sides of the tin.

5 Spoon in half the meat mixture, level the surface and cover it with the pasta. Spoon in the remaining meat mixture, level the top and cover the tin with foil.

6 Cook the meat loaf in the preheated oven, 180°C/350°F/Gas Mark 4, for 1 hour, or until the juices run clear and the loaf has shrunk away from the sides of the tin. Pour off any excess fat from the tin and turn the loaf out on a warmed serving dish. Garnish with the salad leaves and serve hot.

Step *4*

Step *5*

Step *6*

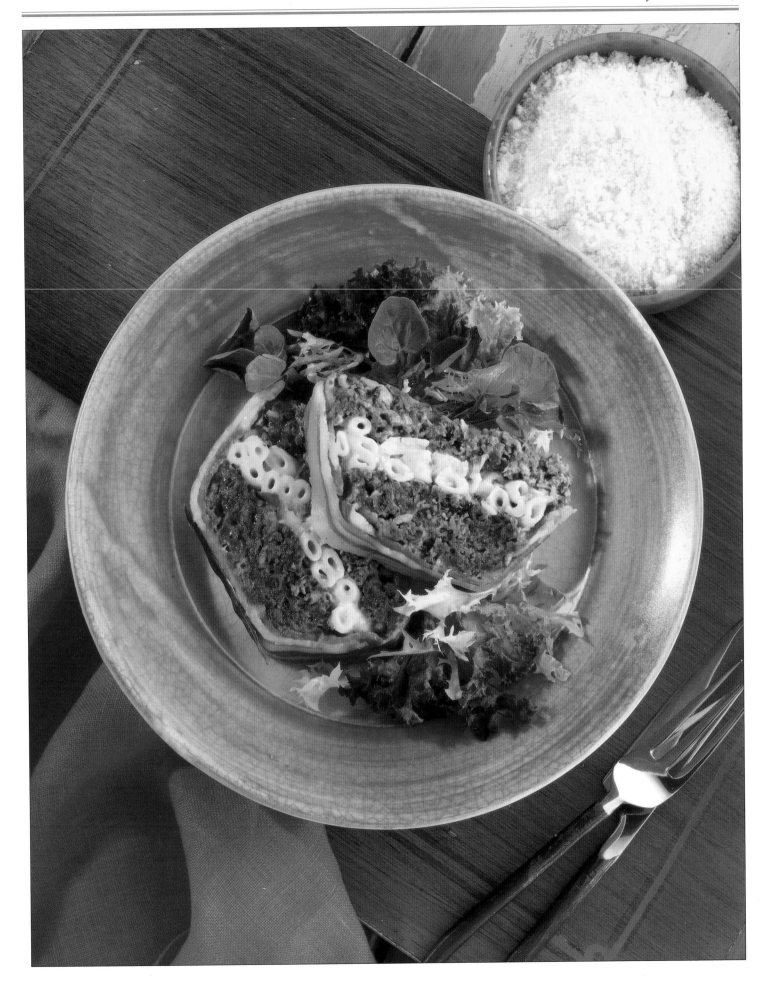

Aubergine (Eggplant) Cake

Layers of toasty-brown aubergine (eggplant), meat sauce and cheese-flavoured pasta make this a popular family supper dish.

SERVES 4

INGREDIENTS

1 aubergine (eggplant), sliced thinly
5 tbsp olive oil
250 g/8 oz short pasta shapes, such as fusilli
60 g/2 oz/¼ cup butter, plus extra for greasing
45 g/1½ oz/6 tbsp flour
300 ml/½ pint/1¼ cups milk
150ml/¼ pint/⅔ cup single (light) cream
150 ml/¼ pint/⅔ cup chicken stock
large pinch of freshly grated nutmeg
90 g/3 oz/¾ cup mature (sharp) Cheddar, grated
30 g/1 oz/¼ cup Parmesan, grated
Lamb Sauce (page 13)
salt and pepper
artichoke heart and tomato salad, to serve

1 Put the aubergine (eggplant) slices in a colander, sprinkle with salt and leave for about 45 minutes. Rinse under cold, running water and drain. Pat dry with paper towels.

2 Heat 4 tablespoons of the oil in a frying pan (skillet) over a medium heat. Fry the aubergine (eggplant) slices for about 4 minutes each side, until golden. Remove with a slotted spoon and drain on paper towels.

3 Meanwhile, cook the pasta in a large pan of boiling salted water, adding 1 tablespoon of olive oil. When the pasta is almost tender, drain it in a colander and return to the pan. Cover and keep warm.

4 Melt the butter in a small pan, stir in the flour and cook for 1 minute. Gradually pour in the milk, stirring all the time, then stir in the cream and chicken stock. Season with nutmeg, salt and pepper, bring to the boil and simmer for 5 minutes. Stir in the Cheddar and remove from the heat. Pour half the sauce over the pasta and mix well. Reserve the remaining sauce.

5 Grease a shallow ovenproof dish. Spoon in half the pasta, cover it with half the lamb sauce and then with the aubergines (eggplant) in a single layer. Repeat the layers of pasta and lamb sauce and spread the remaining cheese sauce over the top. Sprinkle the Parmesan. Bake in the preheated oven, 190°C/375°F/Gas Mark 5, for 25 minutes, until golden brown. Serve hot or cold, with artichoke heart and tomato salad.

Step *2*

Step *4*

Step *5*

Pasticcio

A recipe that has both Italian and Greek origins, this dish may be served hot or cold, cut into thick, satisfying squares.

SERVES 6

INGREDIENTS

250 g/8 oz fusilli, or other short pasta shapes
1 tbsp olive oil
4 tbsp double (heavy) cream
salt
rosemary sprigs, to garnish

SAUCE

2 tbsp olive oil, plus extra for brushing
1 onion, sliced thinly
1 red (bell) pepper, cored, deseeded and chopped
2 cloves garlic, chopped
625 g/1¼ lb minced (ground) lean beef
425 g/14 oz can chopped tomatoes
125 ml/4 fl oz/½ cup dry white wine
2 tbsp chopped fresh parsley
50 g/2 oz can anchovies,
drained and chopped
salt and pepper

TOPPING

300 ml/½ pint/1¼ cups natural yogurt
3 eggs
pinch of freshly grated nutmeg
45 g/1½ oz/⅓ cup Parmesan, grated

1 To make the sauce, heat the oil in a large frying pan (skillet) and fry the onion and red (bell) pepper for 3 minutes. Stir in the garlic and cook for 1 minute more. Stir in the beef and cook, stirring frequently, until no longer pink.

2 Add the tomatoes and wine, stir well and bring to the boil. Simmer, uncovered, for 20 minutes, until the sauce is fairly thick. Stir in the parsley and anchovies, and adjust the seasoning.

3 Cook the pasta in a large pan of boiling salted water, adding the oil. When almost tender, drain in a colander, then transfer to a bowl. Stir in the cream and set aside.

4 To make the topping, beat together the yogurt and eggs and season with nutmeg, and salt and pepper. Stir in the cheese.

5 Brush a shallow baking dish with oil. Spoon in half the macaroni and cover with half the meat sauce. Repeat these layers, spread the topping evenly over the dish and sprinkle on the cheese.

6 Bake in the preheated oven, 190°C/375°F/Gas Mark 5, for 25 minutes, until the topping is golden brown and bubbling. Garnish with rosemary and serve with a selection of raw vegetable crudités.

Step *1*

Step *4*

Step *5*

Tagliatelle with Pumpkin

This unusual pasta dish comes from the Emilia Romagna region.

SERVES 4

INGREDIENTS

500 g/1 lb pumpkin or butternut squash
2 tbsp olive oil
1 onion, chopped finely
2 garlic cloves, crushed
4–6 tbsp chopped fresh parsley
good pinch of ground or freshly grated nutmeg
about 250 ml/8 fl oz/1 cup chicken
or vegetable stock
125 g/4 oz Parma ham (prosciutto),
cut into narrow strips
275 g/9 oz tagliatelle, green or white
(fresh or dried)
150 ml/¼ pint/⅔ cup double (heavy) cream
salt and pepper
freshly grated Parmesan, to serve

1 Peel the pumpkin or butternut squash and scoop out the seeds and membrane. Cut the flesh into 1 cm/ ½ inch dice.

2 Heat the oil in a pan and gently fry the onion and garlic until soft. Add half the parsley and fry for a minute or so longer.

3 Add the pumpkin or squash and continue to cook for 2–3 minutes. Season well with salt, pepper and nutmeg. Add half the stock, bring to the boil, cover and simmer for about 10 minutes or until the pumpkin is tender, adding more stock as necessary. Add the Parma ham (prosciutto) and continue to cook for a further 2 minutes, stirring frequently.

4 Meanwhile, cook the tagliatelle in a large saucepan of boiling salted water, allowing 3–4 minutes for fresh pasta or about 12 minutes for dried (or follow the directions on the packet). When tender but still with some bite, drain thoroughly and turn into a warmed dish.

5 Add the cream to the ham mixture and heat gently until really hot. Adjust the seasoning and spoon over the pasta. Sprinkle with the remaining parsley and grated Parmesan separately.

Step *1*

Step *2*

Step *3*

Tortellini

According to legend, the shape of the tortellini resembles Venus's navel.
When you make tortellini you will know what they should look like!

SERVES 4

INGREDIENTS

FILLING

125 g/4 oz boned and skinned chicken breast
60 g/2 oz Parma ham (prosciutto)
45 g/1½ oz cooked spinach, well drained
1 tbsp finely chopped onion
2 tbsp freshly grated Parmesan
good pinch of ground allspice
1 egg, beaten
salt and pepper
Basic Pasta Dough (page 11)

SAUCE

300 ml/½ pint/1¼ cups single (light) cream
1–2 garlic cloves, crushed
125 g/4 oz button mushrooms, sliced thinly
4 tbsp freshly grated Parmesan
1–2 tbsp chopped fresh parsley

1 Poach the chicken in well-seasoned water until tender, about 10 minutes; drain and chop roughly. When cool put into a food processor with the Parma ham (prosciutto), spinach and onion and process until finely chopped. Stir in the Parmesan, allspice, seasonings and egg.

2 Roll out the pasta dough, half at a time, on a lightly floured surface until as thin as possible. Cut into 4–5 cm/1½–2 inch rounds using a plain cutter.

3 Place ½ teaspoon of the filling in the centre of each dough circle, fold the pieces in half to make a semi-circle and press the edges firmly together. Wrap the semi-circle around your index finger and cross over the two ends, pressing firmly together, curling the rest of the dough backwards to make a 'tummy button' shape. Slip the tortellini off your finger and lay on a lightly floured tray. Repeat with the rest of the dough, re-rolling the trimmings.

4 Heat a large pan of salted boiling water and add a few tortellini. Bring back to the boil and once they rise to the surface cook for about 5 minutes, giving an occasional stir. Remove with a slotted spoon and drain on paper towels. Keep warm in a dish while cooking the remainder.

5 To make the sauce, heat the cream with the garlic in a pan and bring to the boil. Simmer for a few minutes. Add the mushrooms, half the Parmesan and seasoning and simmer for 2–3 minutes. Stir in the parsley and pour over the warm tortellini. Sprinkle the tortellini with the remaining Parmesan and serve immediately.

Step *3*

Step *3*

Step *4*

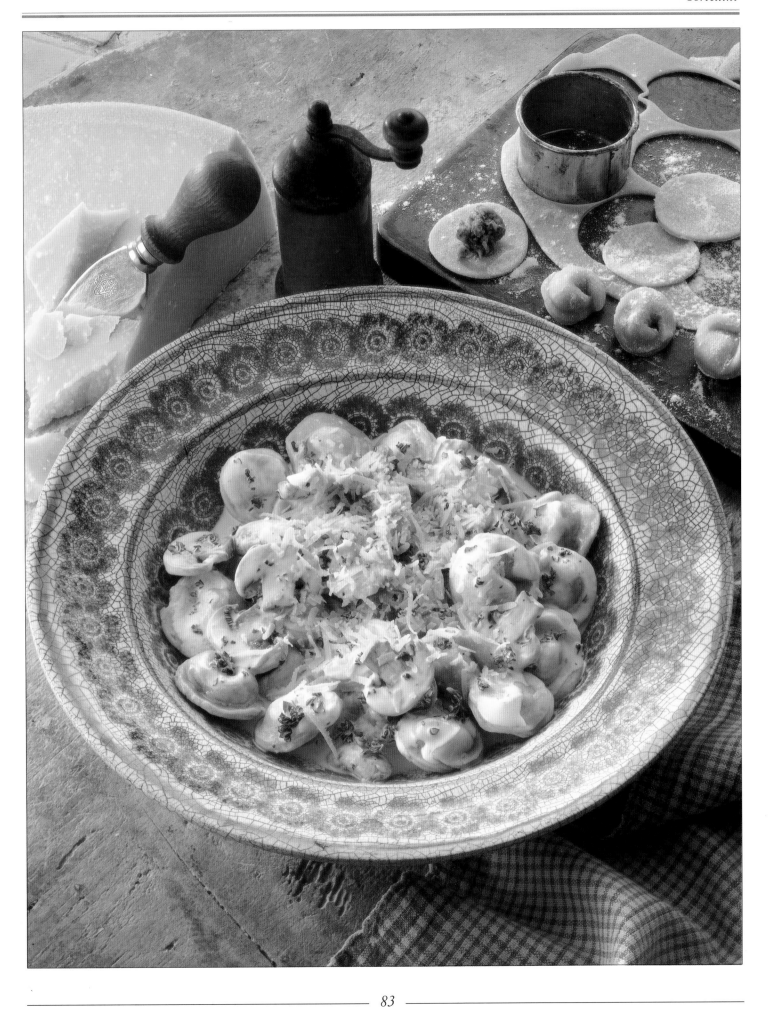

Sicilian Spaghetti

This delicious Sicilian dish originated as a handy way of using up leftover cooked pasta. Any variety of long pasta could be used.

SERVES 4

INGREDIENTS

2 aubergines (eggplant), about 650 g/1¼ lb
150 ml/¼ pint/⅔ cup olive oil
350 g/12 oz finely minced (ground) lean beef
1 onion, chopped
2 garlic cloves, crushed
2 tbsp tomato purée (paste)
425 g/14 oz can chopped tomatoes
1 tsp Worcestershire sauce
1 tsp chopped fresh oregano or marjoram
or ½ tsp dried oregano or marjoram
45 g/1½ oz pitted black olives, sliced
1 green, red or yellow (bell) pepper, cored,
deseeded and chopped
175 g/6 oz spaghetti
125 g/4 oz/1 cup Parmesan, grated
salt and pepper
fresh oregano or parsley, to garnish (optional)

1 Brush a 20 cm/8 inch loose-based round cake tin with olive oil, place a disc of baking parchment in the base and brush with oil. Trim the aubergines (eggplant) and cut into slanting slices, 5 mm/¼ inch thick. Heat some of the oil in a frying pan (skillet). Fry a few slices at a time until lightly browned, turning once, and adding more oil as necessary. Drain on paper towels.

2 Put the minced (ground) beef, onion and garlic into a saucepan and cook, stirring frequently, until browned all over. Add the tomato purée (paste), tomatoes, Worcestershire sauce, herbs and seasoning. Simmer for 10 minutes, stirring occasionally, then add the olives and (bell) pepper and cook for a further 10 minutes.

3 Bring a large pan of salted water to the boil. Cook the spaghetti for 12–14 minutes until just tender. Drain thoroughly. Turn the spaghetti into a bowl and mix in the meat mixture and Parmesan, tossing with two forks.

4 Lay overlapping slices of aubergine (eggplant) evenly over the base of the cake tin and up the sides. Add the meat mixture, pressing it down, and cover with the remaining slices of aubergine (eggplant).

5 Stand in a baking tin and cook in a preheated oven, 200°C/400°F/Gas Mark 6, for 40 minutes. Leave to stand for 5 minutes then loosen around the edges and invert on to a warmed serving dish, releasing the tin clip. Remove the paper. Sprinkle with herbs before serving, if liked. Serve with extra Parmesan, if liked.

Step *1*

Step *3*

Step *4*

Spaghetti with Seafood Sauce

*Frozen shelled prawns (shrimp) from the freezer can become the star
ingredient in this colourful and tasty dish.*

SERVES 4

INGREDIENTS

250 g/8 oz short-cut spaghetti, or long
spaghetti broken into 15 cm/6 inch lengths
2 tbsp olive oil
300 ml/½ pint/1¼ cups chicken stock
1 tsp lemon juice
1 small cauliflower, cut into florets
2 carrots, sliced thinly
125 g/4 oz mangetout (snow peas), trimmed
60 g/2 oz/¼ cup butter
1 onion, sliced
250 g/8 oz courgettes (zucchini), sliced thinly
1 garlic clove, chopped
350 g/12 oz frozen shelled prawns
(shrimp), defrosted
2 tbsp chopped fresh parsley
30 g/1 oz/¼ cup Parmesan, grated
salt and pepper
½ tsp paprika, to sprinkle
4 unshelled prawns (shrimp),
to garnish (optional)

1 Cook the spaghetti in a large pan of boiling salted water, adding 1 tablespoon of the olive oil. When almost tender, drain, then return to the pan and stir in the remaining olive oil. Cover and keep warm.

2 Bring the chicken stock and lemon juice to the boil. Add the cauliflower and carrots and cook for 3–4 minutes until they are barely tender. Remove with a slotted spoon and set aside. Add the mangetout (snow peas) and cook for 1–2 minutes, until they begin to soften. Remove with a slotted spoon and add to the other vegetables. Reserve the stock for future use.

3 Melt half the butter in a frying pan (skillet) over medium heat and fry the onion and courgettes (zucchini) for about 3 minutes. Add the garlic and prawns (shrimp) and cook for a further 2–3 minutes until thoroughly heated through.

4 Stir in the reserved vegetables and heat through. Season well then stir in the remaining butter.

5 Transfer the spaghetti to a warmed serving dish. Pour on the sauce and parsley. Toss well using two forks, until thoroughly coated. Sprinkle on the grated cheese and paprika, and garnish with unshelled prawns (shrimp), if using. Serve immediately.

Step *2*

Step *3*

Step *4*

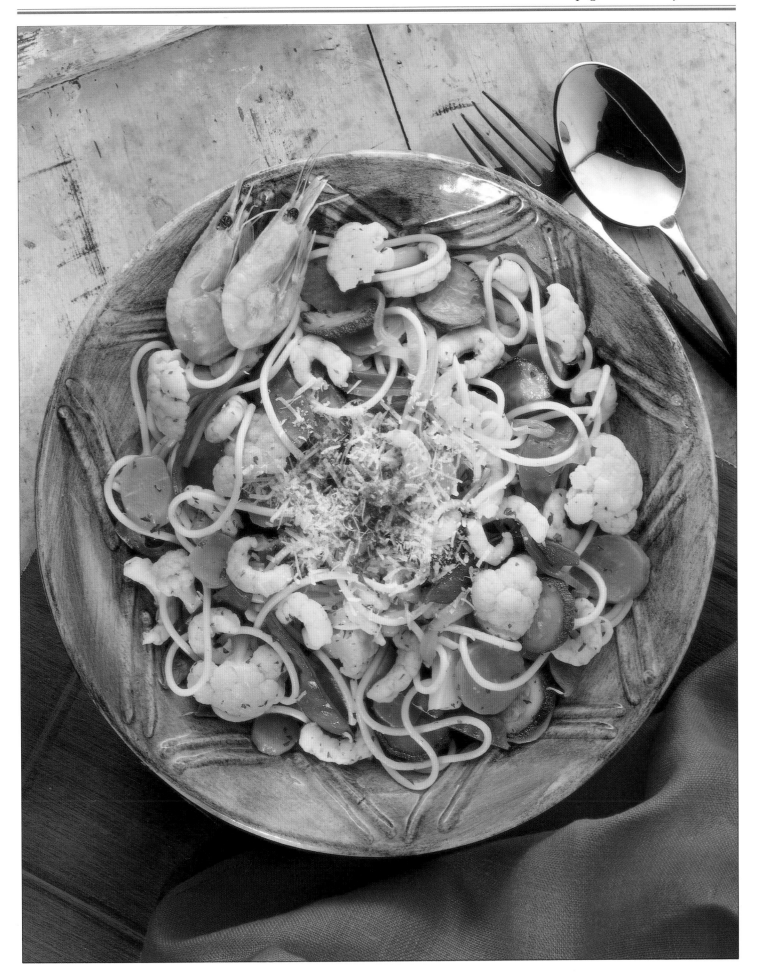

Steamed Pasta Pudding

*A tasty mixture of creamy fish and pasta cooked in a bowl, unmoulded
and drizzled with tomato sauce presents macaroni in a new guise.*

SERVES 4

INGREDIENTS

125 g/4 oz short-cut macaroni, or other
short pasta shapes
1 tbsp olive oil
15 g/½ oz/1 tbsp butter, plus extra for greasing
500 g/1 lb white fish fillets, such as cod,
haddock or coley
a few parsley stalks
6 black peppercorns
125 ml/4 oz/½ cup double (heavy) cream
2 eggs, separated
2 tbsp chopped fresh dill, or parsley
freshly ground black pepper
pinch of freshly grated nutmeg
60 g/2 oz/½ cup Parmesan, grated
Basic Tomato Sauce (page 13), to serve
dill or parsley sprigs, to garnish

1 Cook the pasta in a large pan of salted boiling water, adding the oil. Drain in a colander, return to the pot, add the butter and cover the pan. Keep warm.

2 Place the fish in a frying pan with the parsley stalks, peppercorns and just enough water to cover. Bring to the boil, cover, and simmer for 10 minutes. Lift out the fish with a fish slice, reserving the liquor. When the fish is cool enough to handle, skin and remove any remaining bones. Cut into bite-sized pieces.

3 Transfer the pasta to a large bowl and stir in the cream, egg yolks and dill. Stir in the fish, taking care not to break it up, and enough liquor to make a moist but firm mixture. It should fall easily from a spoon but not be too runny. Whisk the egg whites until stiff but not dry, then fold into the mixture.

4 Grease a heatproof bowl or pudding basin and spoon in the mixture to within 4 cm/1½ inches of the rim. Cover the top with greased greaseproof paper and a cloth, or with foil, and tie firmly around the rim. Do not use foil if you cook the pudding in a microwave.

5 Stand the pudding on a trivet in a large pan of boiling water to come halfway up the sides. Cover and steam for 1½ hours, topping up the boiling water as needed, or cook in a microwave on maximum power for 7 minutes.

6 Run a knife around the inside of the bowl and invert on to a warmed serving dish. Pour some tomato sauce over the top and serve the rest separately. Garnish with the herb sprigs.

Step *2*

Step *3*

Step *5*

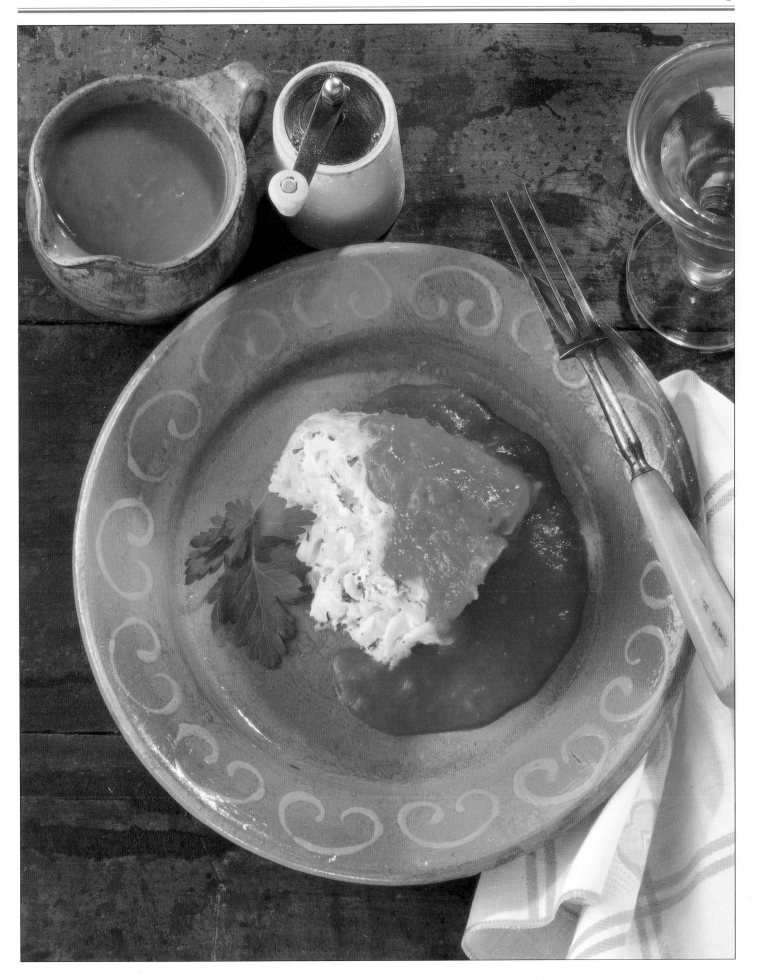

Pasta Shells with Mussels

Serve this aromatic seafood dish to family and friends
who admit to a love of garlic.

SERVES 4–6

INGREDIENTS

425 g/14 oz pasta shells
1 tbsp olive oil

SAUCE

3.5 litres/6 pints mussels, scrubbed
250 ml/8 fl oz/1 cup dry white wine
2 large onions, chopped
125 g/4 oz/½ cup unsalted butter
6 large garlic cloves, chopped finely
5 tbsp chopped fresh parsley
300 ml/½ pint/1¼ cups double (heavy) cream
salt and pepper
crusty bread, to serve

1 Pull off the 'beards' from the mussels and rinse well in several changes of water. Discard any mussels that refuse to close when tapped. Put the mussels in a large pan with the white wine and half the onions. Cover the pan, shake and cook over a medium heat for 2–3 minutes until the mussels open.

2 Remove the pan from the heat, lift out the mussels with a slotted spoon, reserving the liquor, and set aside until they are cool enough to handle. Discard any mussels that have not opened.

3 Melt the butter in a pan over medium heat and fry the remaining onion until translucent. Stir in the garlic and cook for 1 minute more. Gradually pour on the reserved cooking liquor, stirring to blend thoroughly. Stir in the parsley and cream. Season and bring to simmering point. Taste and adjust the seasoning if necessary.

4 Cook the pasta in a large pan of salted boiling water, adding the oil. When it is almost tender, drain in a colander. Return to the pan, cover and keep warm.

5 Remove the mussels from their shells, reserving a few shells for garnish. Stir the mussels into the cream sauce. Tip the pasta into a warmed serving dish, pour on the sauce and, using two large spoons, toss it well. Garnish with a few mussel shells. Serve hot, with warm, crusty bread.

Step *2*

Step *3*

Step *5*

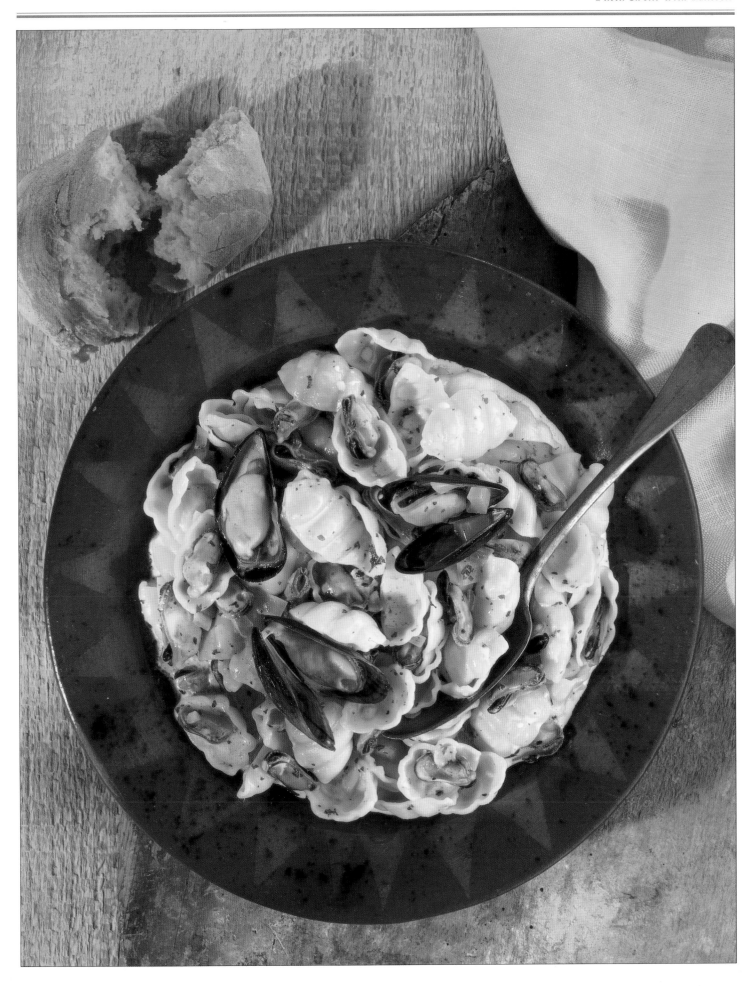

Vermicelli with Clam Sauce

*A quickly cooked recipe that transforms storecupboard ingredients
into a dish with style.*

SERVES 4

INGREDIENTS

425 g/14 oz vermicelli, spaghetti, or
other long pasta
1 tbsp olive oil
30 g/1 oz/2 tbsp butter
2 tbsp Parmesan shavings, to garnish
sprig of basil, to garnish

SAUCE

1 tbsp olive oil
2 onions, chopped
2 garlic cloves, chopped
2 × 200 g/7 oz jars clams in brine
125 ml/4 fl oz/$\frac{1}{2}$ cup white wine
4 tbsp chopped fresh parsley
$\frac{1}{2}$ tsp dried oregano
pinch of freshly grated nutmeg
salt and pepper

1 Cook the pasta in a large pan of boiling salted water, adding the olive oil. When it is almost tender, drain in a colander, return to the pan and add the butter. Cover the pan. Shake it and keep it warm.

2 To make the clam sauce, heat the oil in a pan over a medium heat and fry the onion until it is translucent. Stir in the garlic and cook for 1 further minute.

3 Strain the liquid from one jar of clams, pour into the pan and add the wine. Stir well, bring to simmering point and simmer for 3 minutes. Drain the brine from the second jar of clams and discard.

4 Add the shellfish and herbs to the pan, and season with pepper and nutmeg. Lower the heat and cook until the sauce is heated through.

5 Transfer the pasta to a warmed serving dish and pour on the sauce. Sprinkle with the Parmesan and garnish with the basil sprig. Serve hot.

Step *2*

Step *3*

Step *4*

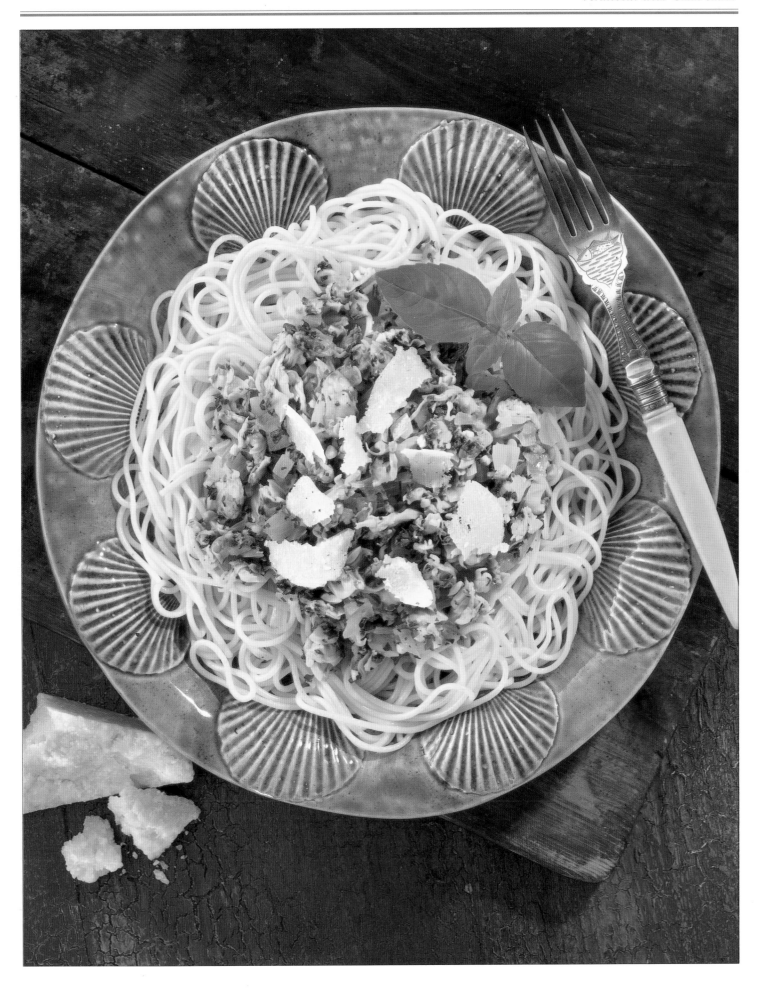

Spaghetti with Smoked Salmon

*Made in moments, this is a dish to astonish and delight
unexpected guests.*

SERVES 4

INGREDIENTS

500 g/1 lb buckwheat spaghetti
2 tbsp olive oil
90 g/3 oz/½ cup feta cheese, crumbled
coriander (cilantro) or parsley, to garnish

SAUCE

300 ml/½ pint/1¼ cups double (heavy) cream
150 ml/¼ pint/⅔ cup whisky or brandy
125 g/4 oz smoked salmon
large pinch of cayenne pepper
2 tbsp chopped coriander (cilantro) or parsley
salt and pepper

1 Cook the spaghetti in a large pan of salted boiling water, adding 1 tablespoon of the olive oil. When the pasta is almost tender, drain in a colander. Return to the pan and sprinkle on the remaining oil. Cover and shake the pan and keep warm.

2 In separate small pans, heat the cream and the whisky or brandy to simmering point. Do not let them boil.

3 Combine the cream with the whisky or brandy. Cut the smoked salmon into thin strips and add to the cream mixture. Season with pepper and cayenne, and stir in the coriander (cilantro) or parsley.

4 Transfer the spaghetti to a warmed serving dish, pour on the sauce and toss thoroughly using two large forks. Scatter the crumbled cheese over the pasta and garnish with the coriander (cilantro) or parsley. Serve at once.

Step *1*

Step *2*

Step *3*

Spaghetti with Tuna & Parsley Sauce

This is a recipe to look forward to when parsley is at its most prolific, in the growing season.

SERVES 4

INGREDIENTS

500 g/1 lb spaghetti
1 tbsp olive oil
30 g/1 oz/2 tbsp butter
black olives, to garnish

SAUCE

200 g/7 oz can tuna, drained
60 g/2 oz can anchovies, drained
250 ml/8 fl oz/1 cup olive oil
250 ml/8 fl oz/1 cup roughly chopped fresh,
flat-leaf parsley
150 ml/¼ pint/⅔ cup crème fraîche
salt and pepper

1 Cook the spaghetti in a large pan of salted boiling water, adding the olive oil. When almost tender, drain in a colander and return to the pan. Add the butter, toss thoroughly to coat and keep warm.

2 Remove any bones from the tuna. Put it into a blender or food processor with the anchovies, olive oil and parsley and process until the sauce is smooth. Pour in the crème fraîche and process for a few seconds to blend. Taste the sauce and season.

3 Warm 4 plates. Shake the pan of spaghetti over medium heat until it is thoroughly warmed through.

4 Pour on the sauce and toss quickly, using two forks. Garnish with the olives and serve immediately with warm, crusty bread.

Step *2*

Step *3*

Step *4*

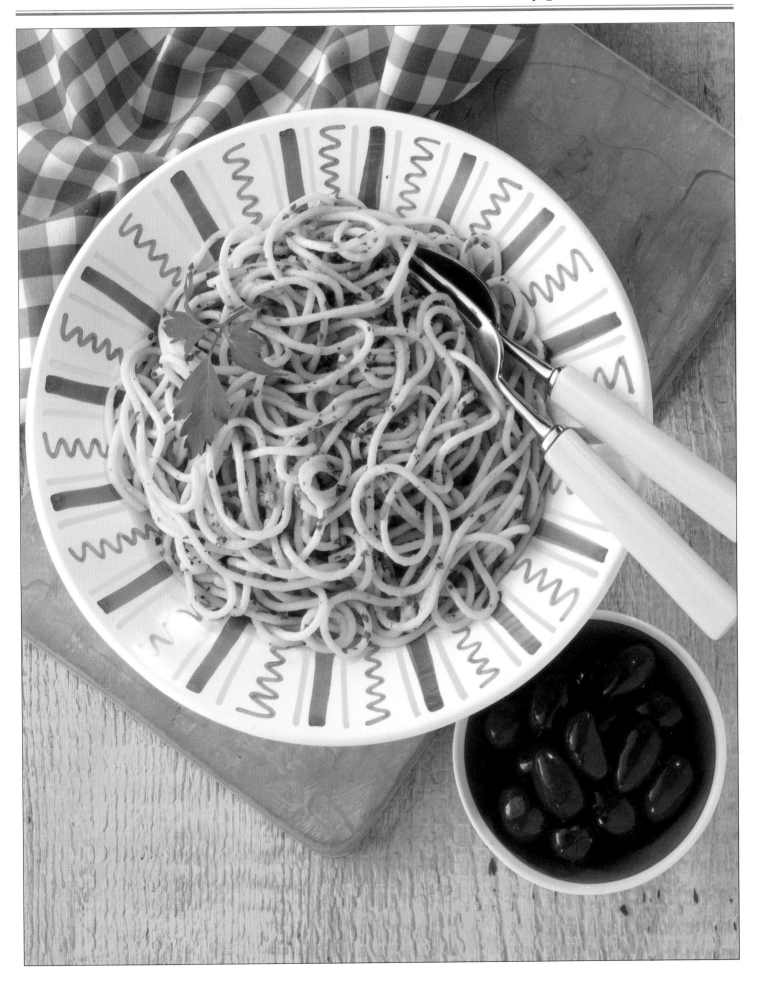

Macaroni & Prawn (Shrimp) Bake

This adaptation of an 18th-century Italian dish is baked until it is golden brown and sizzling, then cut into wedges, like a cake.

SERVES 4

INGREDIENTS

350 g/12 oz short pasta, such as
short-cut macaroni
1 tbsp olive oil, plus extra for brushing
90 g/3 oz/6 tbsp butter, plus extra for greasing
2 small fennel bulbs, sliced thinly,
leaves reserved
175 g/6 oz mushrooms, sliced thinly
175 g/6 oz shelled prawns (shrimp)
60 g/2 oz/½ cup Parmesan, grated
2 large tomatoes, sliced
1 tsp dried oregano
salt and pepper
pinch of cayenne
Béchamel Sauce (page 13)

1 Cook the pasta in a large pan of boiling, salted water with 1 tablespoon of olive oil. When almost tender, drain the pasta in a colander, return to the pan and dot with 30g/1 oz/2 tablespoons of the butter. Shake the pan well, cover and keep warm.

2 Melt the remaining butter in a pan over medium heat and fry the fennel for 3–4 minutes, until it begins to soften. Stir in the mushrooms and fry for a further 2 minutes. Stir in the prawns (shrimp), remove the pan from the heat and set aside.

3 Make the béchamel sauce and add the cayenne. Remove the pan from the heat and stir in the reserved vegetables, prawns (shrimp) and the pasta.

4 Grease a round, shallow baking dish. Pour in the pasta mixture and spread evenly. Sprinkle on the Parmesan, and arrange the tomato slices in a ring around the edge of the dish. Brush the tomato with olive oil and sprinkle on the dried oregano.

5 Bake in the preheated oven, 180°C/350°F/Gas Mark 4, for 25 minutes, until golden brown. Serve hot.

Step *2*

Step *3*

Step *4*

Seafood Lasagne

Layers of cheese sauce, smoked cod and wholewheat lasagne can be assembled overnight and left ready to cook on the following day.

SERVES 6

INGREDIENTS

8 sheets wholewheat lasagne
500 g/1 lb smoked cod
600 ml/1 pint/2½ cups milk
1 tbsp lemon juice
8 peppercorns
2 bay leaves
a few parsley stalks
60 g/2 oz/½ cup mature (sharp) Cheddar, grated
30 g/1 oz/¼ cup Parmesan, grated
salt and pepper
a few whole prawns (shrimp),
to garnish (optional)

SAUCE

60 g/2 oz/¼ cup butter, plus extra for greasing
1 large onion, sliced
1 green (bell) pepper, cored, deseeded
and chopped
1 small courgette (zucchini), sliced
60 g/2 oz/½ cup flour
150 ml/¼ pint/⅔ cup white wine
150 ml/¼ pint/⅔ cup single (light) cream
125 g/4 oz shelled prawns (shrimp)
60 g/2 oz/½ cup mature (sharp) Cheddar, grated

1 Cook the lasagne in boiling, salted water until almost tender, as described on page 70. Drain and reserve.

2 Place the smoked cod, milk, lemon juice, peppercorns, bay leaves and parsley stalks in a frying pan. Bring to the boil, cover and simmer for 10 minutes.

3 Lift the fish from the pan with a slotted spoon. Remove the skin and any bones. Flake the fish. Strain and reserve the liquor.

4 Make the sauce: melt the butter in a pan and fry the onion, (bell) pepper and courgette (zucchini) for 2–3 minutes. Stir in the flour and cook for 1 minute. Gradually add the fish liquor, then stir in the wine, cream and prawns (shrimp). Simmer for 2 minutes. Remove from the heat, add the cheese, and season.

5 Grease a shallow baking dish. Pour in a quarter of the sauce and spread evenly over the base. Cover the sauce with three sheets of lasagne, then with another quarter of the sauce.

6 Arrange the fish on top, then cover with half the remaining sauce. Finish with the remaining lasagne, then the rest of the sauce. Sprinkle the Cheddar and Parmesan over the sauce.

7 Bake in the preheated oven, 190°C/375°F/Gas Mark 5, for 25 minutes, or until the top is golden brown and bubbling. Garnish with a few whole prawns (shrimp), if liked.

Step *2*

Step *5*

Step *6*

Squid & Macaroni Stew

This seafood dish is quick and easy to make, yet is deliciously satisfying to eat.

SERVES 4–6

INGREDIENTS

250 g/8 oz short-cut macaroni, or other
short pasta shapes
1 tbsp olive oil
2 tbsp chopped fresh parsley
salt and pepper

SAUCE

350 g/12 oz cleaned squid, cut into 4 cm/½ in strips
6 tbsp olive oil
2 onions, sliced
250 ml/8 fl oz/1 cup fish stock
150 ml/¼ pint/⅔ cup red wine
350 g/12 oz tomatoes, peeled and
thinly sliced
2 tbsp tomato purée (paste)
1 tsp dried oregano
2 bay leaves

1 Cook the pasta for only 3 minutes in a large pan of boiling salted water, adding the oil. Drain in a colander, return to the pan, cover and keep warm.

2 To make the sauce, heat the oil in a pan over medium heat and fry the onion until translucent. Add the squid and stock and simmer for 5 minutes. Pour on the wine and add the tomatoes, tomato purée (paste), oregano and bay leaves. Bring the sauce to the boil, season and cook, uncovered, for 5 minutes.

3 Add the pasta, stir well, cover the pan and continue simmering it for 10 minutes, or until the macaroni and squid are almost tender. By this time the sauce should be thick and syrupy. If it is too liquid, uncover the pan and continue cooking for a few minutes. Taste the sauce and adjust the seasoning if necessary.

4 Remove the bay leaves and stir in most of the parsley, reserving a little to garnish. Transfer to a warmed serving dish. Sprinkle on the remaining parsley and serve hot. Serve with warm, crusty bread such as ciabatta.

Step *2*

Step *3*

Step *4*

Green Garlic Tagliatelle

A rich pasta dish for garlic lovers everywhere. It's quick and easy to prepare and full of flavour.

SERVES 4

INGREDIENTS

2 tbsp walnut oil
1 bunch spring onions (scallions), sliced
2 garlic cloves, sliced thinly
250 g/8 oz mushrooms, sliced
500 g/1 lb fresh green and white tagliatelle
250 g/8 oz frozen chopped leaf spinach, thawed and drained
125 g/4 oz/½ cup full-fat soft cheese with garlic and herbs
4 tbsp single (light) cream
60 g/2 oz/½ cup chopped, unsalted pistachio nuts
2 tbsp shredded fresh basil
salt and pepper
sprigs of fresh basil, to garnish
Italian bread, to serve

1 Gently heat the oil in a wok or frying pan (skillet) and fry the spring onions (scallions) and garlic for 1 minute until just softened. Add the mushrooms, stir well, cover and cook gently for 5 minutes until softened.

2 Meanwhile, bring a large saucepan of lightly salted water to the boil and cook the pasta for 3–5 minutes until just tender. Drain well and return to the saucepan.

3 Add the spinach to the mushrooms and heat through for 1–2 minutes. Add the cheese and allow to melt slightly. Stir in the cream and continue to heat without allowing to boil.

4 Pour over the pasta, season and mix well. Heat gently, stirring, for 2–3 minutes.

5 Pile into a warmed serving bowl and sprinkle over the pistachio nuts and shredded basil. Garnish with basil sprigs and serve with Italian bread.

Step *1*

Step *3*

Step *4*

Baked Aubergines (Eggplant) with Pasta

Combined with tomatoes and Mozzarella, pasta makes a tasty filling for baked aubergine (eggplant) shells.

SERVES 4

INGREDIENTS:

250 g/8 oz penne, or other short
pasta shapes
4 tbsp olive oil, plus extra for brushing
2 aubergines (eggplant)
1 large onion, chopped
2 garlic cloves, crushed
425 g/14 oz can chopped tomatoes
2 tsp dried oregano
60 g/2 oz Mozzarella, thinly sliced
30 g/1 oz/¼ cup Parmesan, grated
2 tbsp dry breadcrumbs
salt and pepper
salad leaves, to serve

1 Cook the pasta in a large pan of salted boiling water, adding 1 tablespoon of the olive oil. When it is almost tender, drain the pasta in a colander, return to the pan, cover and keep warm.

2 Cut the aubergines (eggplant) in half lengthways. Score around the inside with a knife, then scoop out the flesh with a spoon, taking care not to pierce the skin. Brush the insides of the aubergine (eggplant) shells with olive oil. Chop the flesh and set it aside.

3 Heat the remaining oil in a frying pan over a medium heat and fry the onion until it is translucent. Add the garlic and fry for 1 further minute. Add the chopped aubergine (eggplant) and fry for 5 minutes, stirring frequently. Add the tomatoes and oregano, and season with salt and pepper. Bring to the boil and simmer for 10 minutes, or until the mixture is thick. Taste and adjust the seasoning if necessary. Remove from the heat and stir in the reserved pasta.

4 Brush a baking sheet (cookie sheet) with oil and arrange the aubergine (eggplant) shells in a single layer. Divide half the tomato mixture between the four shells. Arrange the Mozzarella on top and cover with the remaining mixture, piling it into a mound. Mix together the Parmesan and breadcrumbs, and sprinkle over the top, patting it lightly into the mixture.

5 Bake in the preheated oven, 200°C/400°F/Gas Mark 6, for 25 minutes, until the topping is golden brown. Serve hot, with a green salad.

Step *2*

Step *3*

Step *4*

Mediterranean Spaghetti

Delicious Mediterranean vegetables, cooked in a rich tomato sauce, make an ideal topping for nutty wholewheat pasta.

SERVES 4

INGREDIENTS

2 tbsp olive oil
1 large red onion, chopped
2 garlic cloves, crushed
1 tbsp lemon juice
4 baby aubergines (eggplant), quartered
600 ml/1 pint/2½ cups passata (sieved tomatoes)
2 tsp caster (superfine) sugar
2 tbsp tomato purée (paste)
425 g/14 oz can artichoke hearts, drained
and halved
125 g/4 oz/¾ cup pitted black olives
350 g/12 oz wholewheat dried spaghetti
salt and pepper
sprigs of fresh basil, to garnish
olive bread, to serve

1 Heat 1 tablespoon of the oil in a large frying pan (skillet) and gently fry the onion, garlic, lemon juice and aubergines (eggplant) for 4–5 minutes until lightly browned.

2 Pour in the passata, season and add the sugar and tomato purée (paste). Bring to the boil, reduce the heat and simmer for 20 minutes.

3 Gently stir in the artichoke halves and olives and cook for 5 minutes.

4 Meanwhile, bring a large saucepan of lightly salted water to the boil, and cook the spaghetti for 7–8 minutes until just tender. Drain well, toss in the remaining olive oil and season.

5 Pile into a warmed serving bowl and top with the vegetable sauce. Garnish with basil sprigs and serve with olive bread.

Step *1*

Step *2*

Step *3*

Courgette (Zucchini) & Aubergine (Eggplant) Lasagne

This rich, baked pasta dish is packed full of vegetables, tomatoes and Italian Mozzarella cheese.

SERVES 6

INGREDIENTS

1 kg/2 lb aubergines (eggplant)
4 tbsp salt
8 tbsp olive oil
30 g/1 oz/2 tbsp garlic and herb butter
or margarine
500 g/1 lb courgettes (zucchini), sliced
250 g/8 oz/2 cups grated Mozzarella
600 ml/1 pint/2½ cups passata (sieved tomatoes)
6 sheets pre-cooked green lasagne
600 ml/1 pint/2½ cups Béchamel Sauce
(page 13)
60 g/2 oz/½ cup Parmesan, grated
1 tsp dried oregano
black pepper

1 Thinly slice the aubergines (eggplant). Layer the slices in a bowl, sprinkling with the salt as you go. Set aside for 30 minutes. Rinse well in cold water and pat dry with paper towels.

2 Heat 4 tablespoons of the oil in a large frying pan (skillet) until very hot and gently fry half the aubergine (eggplant) slices for 6–7 minutes until lightly golden all over. Drain on paper towels. Repeat with the remaining aubergine slices and oil.

3 Melt the garlic and herb butter or margarine in the frying pan (skillet) and fry the courgettes (zucchini) for 5–6 minutes until golden. Drain on paper towels.

4 Place half the aubergine (eggplant) and courgette (zucchini) slices in a large ovenproof dish. Season with pepper and sprinkle over half the Mozzarella. Spoon over half the passata and top with three sheets of lasagne.

5 Arrange the remaining aubergine (eggplant) and courgette (zucchini) slices on top. Season with pepper and top with the remaining Mozzarella and passata and another layer of lasagne.

6 Spoon over the béchamel sauce and top with Parmesan and oregano. Put on a baking sheet (cookie sheet) and bake in a preheated oven, 220°C/425°F/Gas Mark 7, for 30–35 minutes until golden.

Step *3*

Step *5*

Step *6*

Tricolour Timballini

An unusual way of serving pasta, these cheesy moulds are excellent served with a crunchy salad for a light lunch.

SERVES 4

INGREDIENTS

15 g/½ oz/1 tbsp butter or margarine, softened
60 g/2 oz/½ cup dried white breadcrumbs
175 g/6 oz tricolour spaghetti
300 ml/½ pint/1¼ cups Béchamel Sauce
(page 13)
1 egg yolk
125 g/4 oz/1 cup Gruyère (Swiss) cheese, grated
salt and pepper
fresh flat-leaf parsley, to garnish

SAUCE

2 tsp olive oil
1 onion, chopped finely
1 bay leaf
150 ml/¼ pint/⅔ cup dry white wine
150 ml/¼ pint/⅔ cup passatta (sieved tomatoes)
1 tbsp tomato purée (paste)

1 Grease four 180 ml/6 fl oz/¾ cup moulds or ramekins with the butter or margarine. Evenly coat the insides with half the breadcrumbs.

2 Break the spaghetti into 5 cm/2 inch lengths. Bring a saucepan of lightly salted water to the boil and cook the spaghetti for 5–6 minutes until just tender. Drain well and put in a bowl.

3 Mix the béchamel sauce, egg yolk, cheese and seasoning into the cooked pasta and pack into the moulds.

4 Sprinkle with the remaining breadcrumbs and put on a baking sheet (cookie sheet). Bake in a preheated oven, 220°C/425°F/Gas Mark 7, for 20 minutes until golden. Leave to stand for 10 minutes.

5 Meanwhile, make the sauce. Heat the oil in a saucepan and gently fry the onion and bay leaf for 2–3 minutes until just softened.

6 Stir in the wine, passata, tomato purée (paste) and seasoning. Bring to the boil and simmer for 20 minutes until thickened. Discard the bay leaf.

7 Run a palette knife (spatula) around the inside of the moulds or ramekins. Turn on to serving plates, garnish and serve with the tomato sauce.

Step *2*

Step *3*

Step *4*

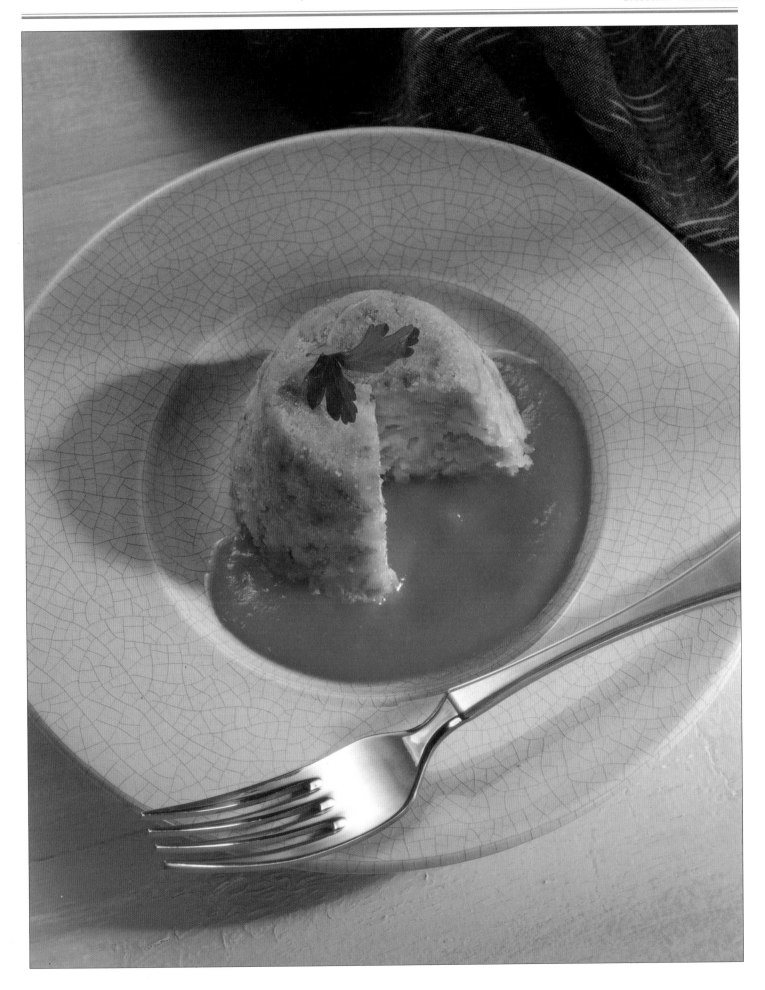

Vegetable Pasta Stir-Fry

Prepare all the vegetables and cook the pasta in advance,
then the dish can be cooked in a few minutes.

SERVES 4

INGREDIENTS

425 g/14 oz wholewheat pasta shells, or other
short pasta shapes
1 tbsp olive oil
2 carrots, sliced thinly
125 g/4 oz baby sweetcorn
3 tbsp peanut oil
2.5 cm/1 inch ginger root, sliced thinly
1 large onion, sliced thinly
1 garlic clove, sliced thinly
3 celery stalks, sliced thinly
1 small red (bell) pepper, cored, deseeded and
sliced into matchstick strips
1 small green (bell) pepper, cored, deseeded
and sliced into matchstick strips
salt
steamed mangetout (snow peas), to serve

SAUCE

1 tsp cornflour (cornstarch)
2 tbsp water
3 tbsp soy sauce
3 tbsp dry sherry
1 tsp clear honey
few drops of hot pepper sauce (optional)

1 Cook the pasta in a large pan of boiling salted water, adding the tablespoon of olive oil. When almost tender, drain the pasta in a colander, return to the pan, cover and keep warm.

2 Cook the carrots and sweetcorn in boiling, salted water for 2 minutes. Drain in a colander, plunge into cold water to prevent further cooking and drain again.

3 Heat the peanut oil in a wok or large frying pan (skillet) over medium heat and fry the ginger for 1 minute, to flavour the oil. Remove with a slotted spoon and discard.

4 Add the onion, garlic, celery and (bell) peppers to the oil and stir-fry for 2 minutes. Add the carrots and sweetcorn, and stir-fry for a further 2 minutes, then stir in the reserved pasta.

5 Put the cornflour (cornstarch) in a small bowl and mix to a smooth paste with the water. Stir in the soy sauce, sherry and honey.

6 Pour the sauce into the pan, stir well and cook for 2 minutes, stirring once or twice. Taste the sauce and season with hot pepper sauce if liked. Serve with a steamed green vegetable such as mangetout (snow peas).

Step *3*

Step *4*

Step *6*

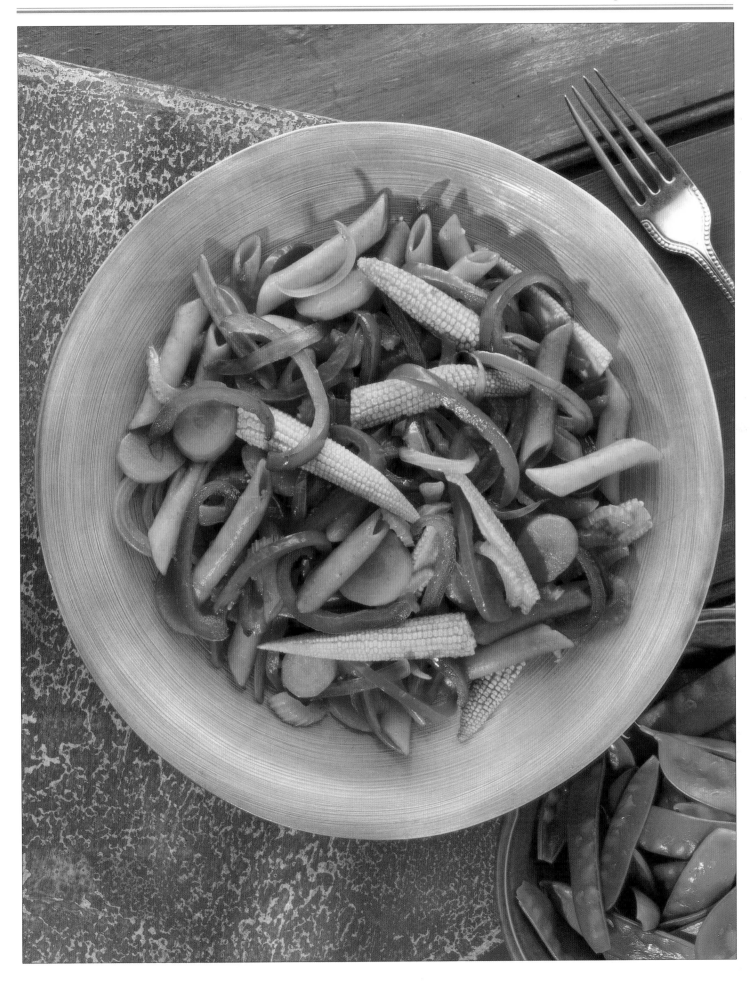

Pasta with Green Vegetable Sauce

The different shapes and textures of the vegetables make a mouthwatering presentation in this light and summery dish.

SERVES 4

INGREDIENTS

250 g/8 oz gemelli or other pasta shapes
1 tbsp olive oil
2 tbsp chopped fresh parsley
2 tbsp freshly grated Parmesan
salt and pepper

SAUCE

1 head green broccoli, cut into florets
2 courgettes (zucchini), sliced
250 g/8 oz asparagus spears, trimmed
125 g/4 oz mangetout (snow peas), trimmed
125 g/4 oz frozen peas
30 g/1 oz/2 tbsp butter
3 tbsp vegetable stock
5 tbsp double (heavy) cream
large pinch of freshly grated nutmeg

1 Cook the pasta in a large pan of salted boiling water, adding the olive oil. When almost tender, drain in a colander and return to the pan, cover and keep warm.

2 Steam the broccoli, courgettes (zucchini), asparagus spears and mangetout (snow peas) over a pan of boiling, salted water until just beginning to soften. Remove from the heat and plunge into cold water to prevent further cooking. Drain and set aside.

3 Cook the peas in boiling, salted water for 3 minutes, then drain. Refresh in cold water and drain again.

4 Put the butter and vegetable stock in a pan over a medium heat. Add all the vegetables except the asparagus spears and toss carefully with a wooden spoon to heat through, taking care not to break them up.

5 Stir in the cream, allow the sauce just to heat through and season well with salt, pepper and nutmeg.

6 Transfer the pasta to a warmed serving dish and stir in the chopped parsley. Spoon the sauce over, and sprinkle on the Parmesan. Arrange the asparagus spears in a pattern on top. Serve hot.

Step *2*

Step *4*

Step *5*

Vegetarian Pasta & Bean Casserole

A satisfying winter dish, this vegetable, pasta and bean casserole with a crunchy topping is a slow-cooked, one-pot meal.

SERVES 6

INGREDIENTS

250 g/8 oz/generous 1 cup dried
haricot beans, soaked overnight and drained
250 g/8 oz penne, or other short pasta shapes
6 tbsp olive oil
900 ml/1½ pints/3½ cups vegetable stock
2 large onions, sliced
2 cloves garlic, chopped
2 bay leaves
1 tsp dried oregano
1 tsp dried thyme
5 tbsp red wine
2 tbsp tomato purée (paste)
2 celery stalks, sliced
1 fennel bulb, sliced
125 g/4 oz mushrooms, sliced
250 g/8 oz tomatoes, sliced
1 tsp dark muscovado sugar
4 tbsp dry white breadcrumbs
salt and pepper

TO SERVE

salad leaves
crusty bread

1 Put the beans in a large pan, cover them with water and bring to the boil. Boil the beans rapidly for 20 minutes, then drain them.

2 Cook the pasta for only 3 minutes in a large pan of boiling salted water, adding 1 tablespoon of the oil. Drain in a colander and set aside.

3 Put the beans in a large flameproof casserole, pour on the vegetable stock and stir in the remaining olive oil, the onions, garlic, bay leaves, herbs, wine and tomato purée (paste).

4 Bring to the boil, cover the casserole and cook in a preheated oven, 180°C/350°F/Gas Mark 4, for 2 hours.

5 Add the reserved pasta, the celery, fennel, mushrooms and tomatoes, and season with salt and pepper.

6 Stir in the sugar and sprinkle on the breadcrumbs. Cover the casserole and continue cooking for another hour. Serve hot, with salad leaves and plenty of crusty bread.

Step *3*

Step *5*

Step *6*

Vermicelli Flan

Lightly cooked vermicelli is pressed into a flan ring and baked with a creamy mushroom filling.

SERVES 4

INGREDIENTS

250 g/8 oz vermicelli or spaghetti
1 tbsp olive oil
30 g/1 oz/2 tbsp butter, plus extra for greasing
salt
tomato and basil salad, to serve

SAUCE

60 g/2 oz/¼ cup butter
1 onion, chopped
150 g/5 oz button mushrooms, trimmed
1 green (bell) pepper, cored, deseeded and
sliced into thin rings
150 ml/¼ pint/⅔ cup milk
3 eggs, beaten lightly
2 tbsp double (heavy) cream
1 tsp dried oregano
pinch of finely grated nutmeg
freshly ground black pepper
1 tbsp freshly grated Parmesan

1 Cook the pasta in a large pan of salted boiling water, adding the olive oil. When almost tender, drain in a colander. Return the pasta to the pan, add the butter and shake the pan well.

2 Grease a 20 cm/8 inch loose-bottomed flan tin (pan). Press the pasta on to the base and round the sides to form a case.

3 Heat the butter in a frying pan (skillet) over a medium heat and fry the onion until it is translucent. Remove with a slotted spoon and spread in the flan base.

4 Add the mushrooms and (bell) pepper rings to the pan and turn them in the fat until glazed. Fry for two minutes on each side, then arrange in the flan base.

5 Beat together the milk, eggs and cream, stir in the oregano, and season with nutmeg and pepper. Pour the mixture carefully over the vegetables and sprinkle on the cheese.

6 Bake the flan in the preheated oven, 180°C/350°F/Gas Mark 4, for 40–45 minutes, until filling is set. Slide on to a serving plate and serve warm.

Step *3*

Step *4*

Step *5*

FISH DISHES

Italians eat everything that comes out of the sea, from the smallest whitebait to the massive tuna fish. Fish markets in Italy are fascinating, with a huge variety of fish on display, but as most of the fish comes from the Mediterranean it is not always easy to find an equivalent elsewhere. However, fresh or frozen import-ed fish of all kinds is increasingly appearing in fishmongers and supermarkets.

After pasta, fish is probably the most important source of food in Italy, and in many recipes fish or seafood are combined with one type of pasta or another.

The inland regions of Italy, such as Lombardy and Umbria, have lakes with plentiful supplies of fish while Apulia has abundant supplies caught by offshore trawlers. The south has splendid fish with tuna and swordfish taking pride of place, although red mullet and sea bass are plentiful and popular too. Venice and surrounding areas have a wealth of fish and seafood recipes, often combined with pasta. The Ligurian coast is well-known for its fish soups and stews. The islands of Sicily and Sardinia abound with fish which feature widely in their cuisine, including the sardines which give Sardinia its name.

Squid Casserole

Squid is often served fried in Italy, but here it is casseroled with tomatoes and (bell) peppers to give a rich sauce.

SERVES 4

INGREDIENTS

1 kg/2 lb whole squid, cleaned or 750 g/1½ lb
squid rings, defrosted if frozen
3 tbsp olive oil
1 large onion, sliced thinly
2 garlic cloves, crushed
1 red (bell) pepper, cored, deseeded and sliced
1–2 sprigs fresh rosemary
150 ml/¼ pint/⅔ cup dry white wine and
250 ml/8 fl oz/1 cup water, or
350 ml/12 fl oz/1½ cups water or fish stock
425 g/14 oz can chopped tomatoes
2 tbsp tomato purée (paste)
1 tsp paprika
salt and pepper
fresh sprigs of rosemary or parsley, to garnish

1 Cut the squid pouch into 1 cm/½ inch slices; cut the tentacles into lengths of about 5 cm/2 inches. If using frozen squid rings, make sure they are fully defrosted and well drained.

2 Heat the oil in a flameproof casserole and fry the onion and garlic gently until soft. Add the squid, increase the heat and continue to cook for about 10 minutes until sealed and beginning to colour lightly. Add the red (bell) pepper, rosemary and wine (if using), and water or stock and bring up to the boil. Cover and simmer gently for 45 minutes.

3 Discard the sprigs of rosemary (but don't take out any leaves that have come off). Add the tomatoes, tomato purée (paste), seasonings and paprika. Continue to simmer gently for 45–60 minutes, or cover the casserole tightly and cook in a moderate oven, 180°C/350°F/Gas Mark 4, for 45–60 minutes until tender.

4 Give the sauce a good stir, adjust the seasoning and serve with crusty bread.

Step *1*

Step *2*

Step *3*

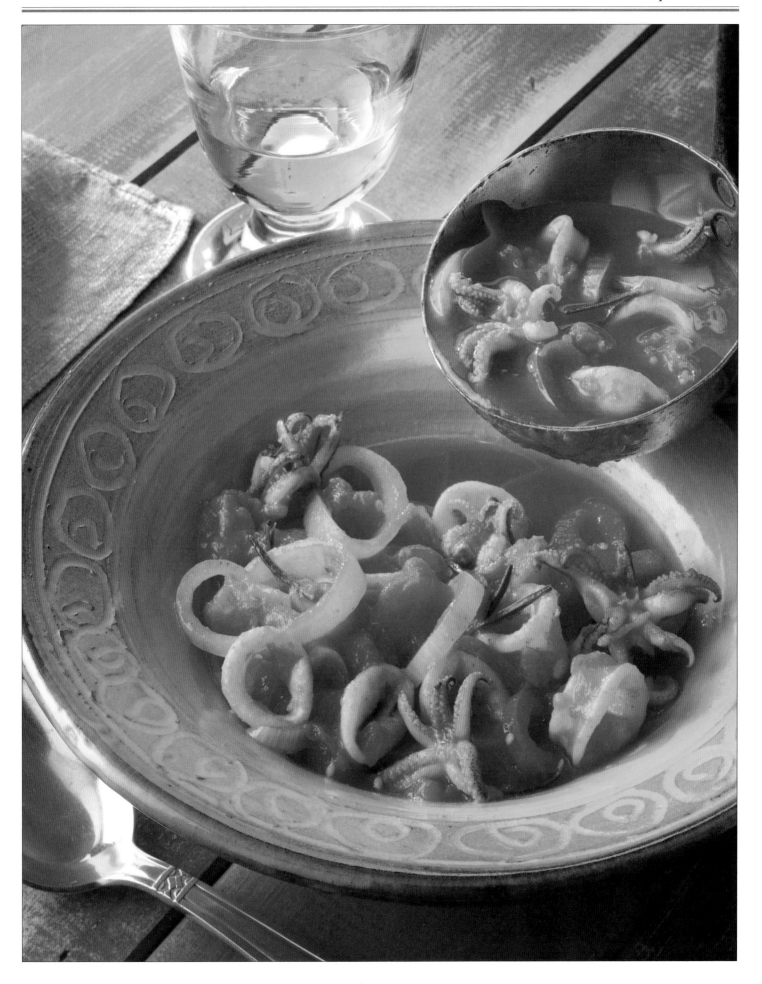

Baked Sea Bass

Sea bass is a delicious white-fleshed fish. If cooking two small fish, they can be grilled (broiled); if cooking one large fish, bake it in the oven.

SERVES 4

INGREDIENTS

1.4 kg/3 lb fresh sea bass or
2 x 750 g/1½ lb sea bass, gutted
2–4 sprigs fresh rosemary
½ lemon, sliced thinly
2 tbsp olive oil

GARLIC SAUCE

2 tsp coarse sea salt
2 tsp capers
2 garlic cloves, crushed
4 tbsp water
2 fresh bay leaves
1 tsp lemon juice or wine vinegar
2 tbsp olive oil
pepper

TO GARNISH

bay leaves
lemon wedges

1 Scrape off the scales from the fish and cut off the sharp fins. Make diagonal cuts along both sides. Wash and dry thoroughly. Place a sprig of rosemary in the cavity of each of the smaller fish with half the lemon slices; or two sprigs and all the lemon in the large fish.

2 To grill (broil), place in a foil-lined pan, brush lightly with 1–2 tablespoons oil and grill (broil) under a moderate heat for about 5 minutes each side or until cooked through, turning carefully.

3 To bake: place the fish in a foil-lined dish or roasting tin brushed with oil, and brush the fish with the rest of the oil. Cook in a preheated oven, 190°C/375°F/Gas Mark 5 for about 30 minutes for the small fish or 45–50 minutes for the large fish, until the thickest part of the fish is opaque.

4 For the sauce: crush the salt and capers with the garlic in a pestle and mortar if available and then gradually work in the water. Alternatively, put it all into a food processor or blender and switch on until smooth.

5 Bruise the bay leaves and remaining sprigs of rosemary and put in a bowl. Add the garlic mixture, lemon juice or vinegar and oil and pound together until the flavours are released. Season with pepper.

6 Place the fish on a serving dish and, if liked, carefully remove the skin. Spoon some of the sauce over the fish and serve the rest separately. Garnish with fresh bay leaves and lemon wedges.

Step *1*

Step *4*

Step *5*

Trout in Red Wine

This recipe from Trentino is best when the fish are freshly caught, but it is a good way to cook any trout, giving it an interesting flavour.

SERVES 4

INGREDIENTS

4 fresh trout, about 300 g/10 oz each
250 ml/8 fl oz/1 cup red or white wine vinegar
300 ml/½ pint/1¼ cups red or dry white wine
150 ml/¼ pint/ ⅔ cup water
1 carrot, sliced
2–4 bay leaves
thinly pared rind of 1 lemon
1 small onion, sliced very thinly
4 sprigs fresh parsley
4 sprigs fresh thyme
1 tsp black peppercorns
6–8 whole cloves
90 g/3 oz/6 tbsp butter
1 tbsp chopped fresh mixed herbs
salt and pepper

TO GARNISH

sprigs of herbs
lemon slices

1 Gut the trout but leave their heads on. Dry on paper towels and lay the fish head to tail in a shallow container or baking tin just large enough to hold them.

2 Bring the wine vinegar to the boil and pour slowly all over the fish. Leave the fish to marinate in the refrigerator for about 20 minutes.

3 Put the wine, water, carrot, bay leaves, lemon rind, onion, herbs, peppercorns and cloves into a pan with a good pinch of sea salt and heat gently.

4 Drain the fish thoroughly, discarding the vinegar. Place the fish in a fish kettle or large frying pan (skillet) so they touch. When the wine mixture boils, strain gently over the fish so they are about half covered. Cover the pan and simmer very gently for 15 minutes.

5 Carefully remove the fish from the pan, draining off as much of the liquid as possible, and arrange on a serving dish. Keep warm.

6 Boil the cooking liquid hard until reduced to about 4–6 tablespoons. Melt the butter in a small saucepan and strain in the cooking liquor. Adjust the seasoning and spoon over the fish. Sprinkle with chopped mixed herbs and garnish with lemon and sprigs of herbs.

Step *1*

Step *3*

Step *4*

Sardine & Potato Bake

Fresh sardines are now readily available, so this traditional dish from
Liguria can be enjoyed by all.

SERVES 4

INGREDIENTS

1 kg/2 lb potatoes
1 kg/2 lb sardines, defrosted if frozen
1 tbsp olive oil, plus extra for oiling
1 onion, chopped
2–3 garlic cloves, crushed
2 tbsp chopped fresh parsley
350 g/12 oz ripe tomatoes, peeled and sliced
or 425 g/14 oz can peeled tomatoes, partly drained
and chopped
1–2 tbsp chopped fresh Italian herbs, such as
oregano, thyme, rosemary, marjoram
150 ml/¼ pint/⅔ cup dry white wine
salt and pepper

1 Put the potatoes in a pan of salted water, bring to the boil, cover and simmer for 10 minutes then drain. When cool enough to handle, cut into slices about 5 mm/¼ inch thick.

2 Gut and clean the sardines: cut off their heads and tails and then slit open the length of the belly. Turn the fish over so the skin is upwards and press firmly along the backbone to loosen the bones. Turn over again and carefully remove the backbone. Wash the fish in cold water, drain well and dry them on paper towels.

3 Heat the oil in a pan and fry the onion and garlic until soft, but not coloured.

4 Arrange the potatoes in a well-oiled ovenproof dish and sprinkle with the onions and then the parsley and plenty of seasoning.

5 Lay the open sardines over the potatoes, skin-side down, then cover with the tomatoes and the rest of the herbs. Pour on the wine and season again.

6 Cook uncovered in a preheated oven, 190°C/180°F/ Gas Mark 5, for about 40 minutes until the fish is tender. If the casserole seems to be drying out, add another couple of tablespoons of wine.

Step *2*

Step *4*

Step *5*

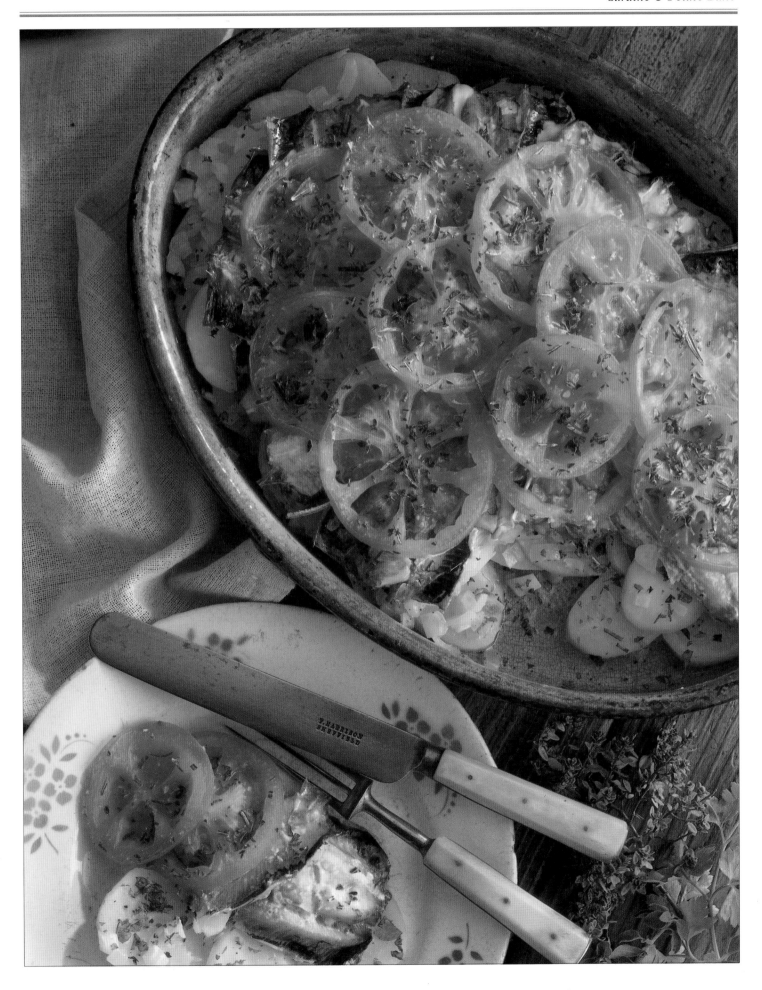

Skewered Monkfish with Caper Sauce

*Monkfish is a very meaty-textured fish. It cooks very
well as it doesn't flake like most other fish.*

SERVES 4

INGREDIENTS

750 g/1¹/₂ lb monkfish tail
finely grated rind and juice 1 small lemon
2 tbsp olive oil
a small bunch of fresh bay leaves
1 small lemon, cut into wedges

FOR THE SAUCE

6 tbsp olive oil
1 garlic clove, chopped finely
finely grated rind and juice 1 small lemon
1 tbsp chopped fresh parsley
2 tbsp capers, drained and chopped
3 anchovy fillets, chopped finely
pepper

1 Wash and pat dry the monkfish using paper towels. Carefully trim away the pinky grey membrane and slice either side the central bone to give 2 thick fillets.

2 Cut the monkfish into 2.5 cm/ 1 inch cubes and place in a shallow dish. Toss in the lemon rind and juice and the olive oil.

3 Drain the fish, reserving the juices, and thread on to four bamboo skewers, threading a few bay leaves and wedges of lemon in between the fish cubes.

4 Preheat a grill (broiler) to medium. Place the skewers on a rack and cover the ends of the skewers with foil to prevent burning. Brush with some of the reserved juices and cook for 3 minutes. Turn over, brush again and cook for a further 3–4 minutes until tender and cooked through.

5 Meanwhile, mix together all the ingredients for the sauce and set aside.

6 Drain the skewers and transfer to warmed serving plates. Serve with the sauce and a green salad.

Step *1*

Step *3*

Step *5*

Pan-Fried Prawns (Shrimp) with Garlic

A luxurious dish which makes an impressive starter or light meal.

SERVES 4

INGREDIENTS

4 garlic cloves
20–24 unshelled large raw prawns (shrimp)
125 g/4 oz/8 tbsp butter
4 tbsp olive oil
6 tbsp brandy
salt and pepper
2 tbsp chopped fresh parsley

1 Peel and slice the garlic.

2 Wash the prawns (shrimp) and pat dry using paper towels.

3 Melt the butter with the oil in a large frying pan (skillet), add the garlic and prawns (shrimp), and fry over a high heat, stirring, for 3–4 minutes until the prawns (shrimp) are pink.

4 Sprinkle with brandy and season to taste. Sprinkle with parsley and serve immediately with lemon wedges and ciabatta bread, if liked.

Step *1*

Step *3*

Step *4*

POULTRY &
MEAT DISHES

*Italians have their own special way of butchering meat,
producing very different cuts. Most meat is sold ready
boned and often cut straight across the grain.
Veal is a great favourite and widely available. Pork is
also popular, with roast pig being the traditional dish of
Umbria. Suckling pig is roasted with lots of fresh herbs,
especially rosemary, until the skin is crisp and brown.
Lamb is often served for special occasions, cooked
on a spit or roasted in the oven with wine, garlic and
herbs; and the very small cutlets from young lambs
feature widely, especially in Rome. Offal plays an
important role, with liver, brains, sweetbreads, tongue,
heart, tripe and kidneys always available. Poultry dishes
provide some of Italy's finest food. Every part of the
chicken is used, including the feet and innards
for making soup. Spit-roasted chicken, flavoured
strongly with rosemary, has become almost a national
dish. Turkey, capon, duck, goose and guinea fowl are
also popular, as is game. Wild rabbit, hare, wild boar
and deer are available, especially in Sardinia.*

Pan-Cooked Chicken with Artichokes

Artichokes are a familiar ingredient in Italian cookery.
In this dish, they are used to delicately flavour chicken.

SERVES 4

INGREDIENTS

4 chicken breasts, part boned
30 g/1 oz/2 tbsp butter
2 tbsp olive oil
2 red onions, cut into wedges
2 tbsp lemon juice
150 ml/¼ pt/⅔ cup dry white wine
150 ml/¼ pt/⅔ cup chicken stock
2 tsp plain flour
425 g/14 oz can artichoke halves,
drained and halved
salt and pepper
chopped fresh parsley, to garnish

1 Season the chicken with salt and freshly ground black pepper. Heat the oil and 15 g/½ oz/1 tablespoon of the butter in a large frying pan (skillet). Add the chicken and fry for 4–5 minutes on each side until lightly golden. Remove from the pan using a slotted spoon.

2 Toss the onion in the lemon juice, and add to the frying pan (skillet). Gently fry, stirring, for 3–4 minutes until just beginning to soften.

3 Return the chicken to the pan. Pour in the wine and stock, bring to the boil, cover and simmer gently for 30 minutes.

4 Remove the chicken from the pan, reserving the cooking juices, and keep warm. Bring the juices to the boil, and boil rapidly for 5 minutes.

5 Blend the remaining butter with the flour to form a paste. Reduce the juices to a simmer and drop the paste into the frying pan (skillet), stirring until thickened.

6 Adjust the seasoning, stir in the artichoke hearts and cook for a further 2 minutes. Pour over the chicken and garnish with parsley.

Step *1*

Step *3*

Step *5*

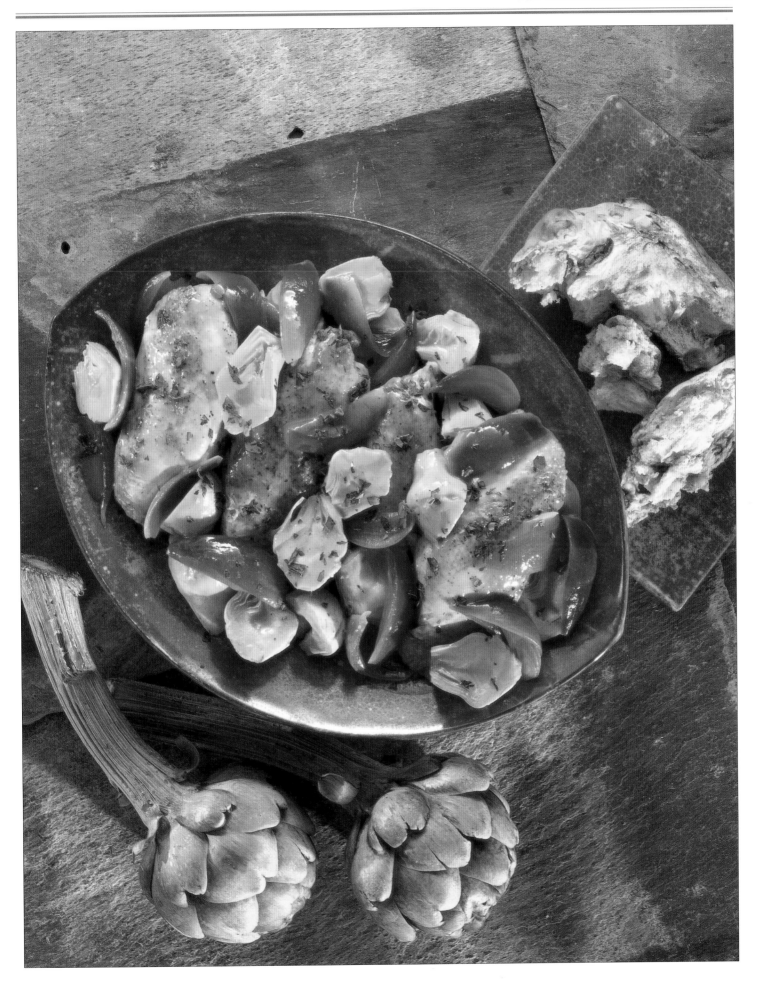

Barbecued Chicken

You need a bit of brute force to prepare the chicken, but once marinated it's an easy and tasty candidate for the barbecue.

SERVES 4

INGREDIENTS

1.5 kg/3 lb chicken
grated rind of 1 lemon
4 tbsp lemon juice
2 sprigs rosemary
1 small red chilli, chopped finely
150 ml/¼ pint/⅔ cup olive oil

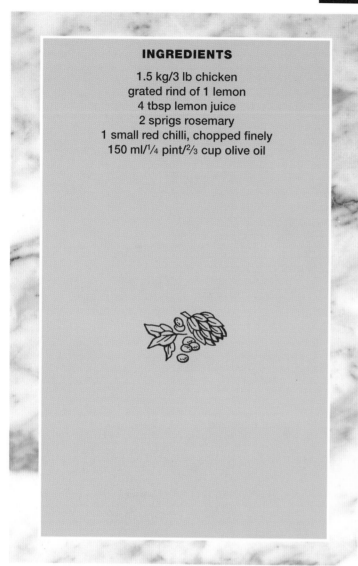

1 Split the chicken down the breast bone and open it out. Trim off excess fat, and remove the parson's nose, wing and leg tips. Break the leg and wing joints to enable you to pound it flat. This ensures that it cooks evenly.

2 Cover the split chicken with clingfilm (plastic wrap) and pound it as flat as possible with a rolling pin.

3 Mix the lemon rind and juice, rosemary sprigs, chilli and olive oil together in a small bowl. Place the chicken in a large dish and pour over the marinade, turning the chicken to coat it evenly. Cover the dish and leave the chicken to marinate for at least 2 hours.

4 Cook the chicken over a hot barbecue (the coals should be white, and red when fanned) for about 30 minutes, turning it regularly until the skin is golden and crisp. To test if it is cooked, pierce one of the chicken thighs; if it is ready, the juices should run clear, not pink. Serve with a salad.

Step *1*

Step *2*

Step *4*

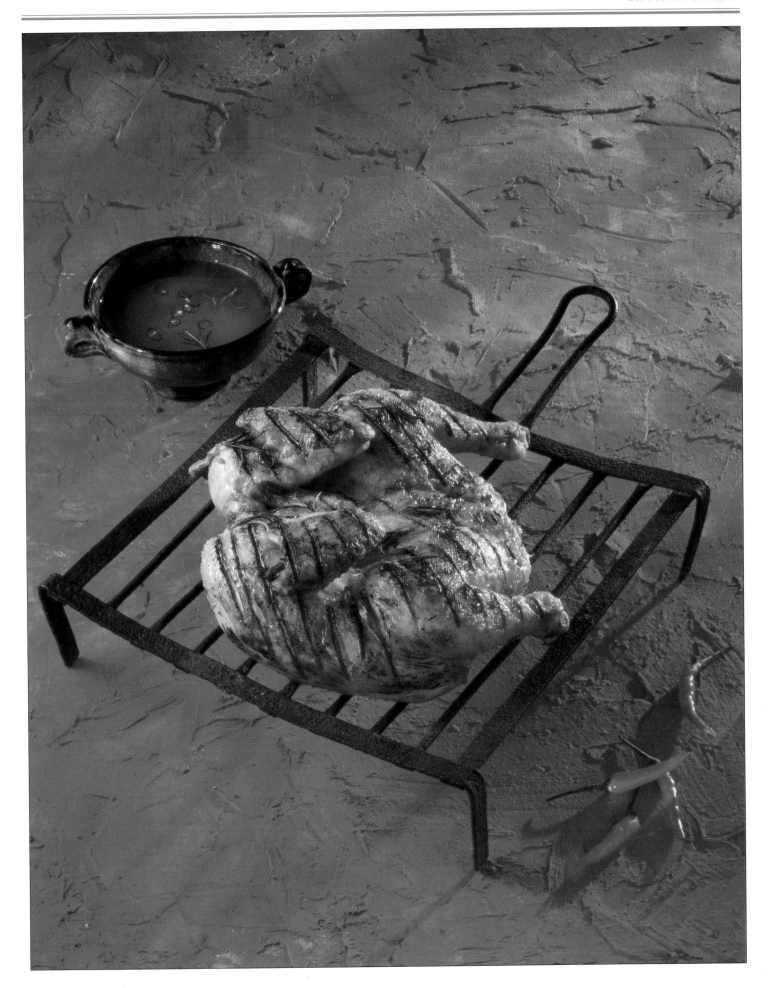

Chicken with Green Olives

Olives are a popular flavouring for poultry and game in Apulia,
where this recipe originates.

SERVES 4

INGREDIENTS

4 chicken breasts, part boned
30 g/1 oz/2 tbsp butter
2 tbsp olive oil
1 large onion, chopped finely
2 garlic cloves, crushed
2 (bell) peppers, red, yellow or green, cored,
deseeded and cut into large pieces
250 g/8 oz large closed cup mushrooms,
sliced or quartered
175 g/6 oz tomatoes, peeled and halved
150 ml/¼ pint/⅔ cup dry white wine
125–175 g/4–6 oz green olives, pitted
4–6 tbsp double (heavy) cream
salt and pepper
chopped flat-leaf parsley, to garnish

1 Season the chicken with salt and pepper. Heat the oil and butter in a frying pan (skillet), add the chicken and fry until browned all over. Remove from the pan.

2 Add the onion and garlic to the pan and fry gently until beginning to soften. Add the (bell) peppers to the pan with the mushrooms and continue to cook for a few minutes longer.

3 Add the tomatoes and plenty of seasoning to the pan and then transfer the vegetable mixture to an ovenproof casserole. Place the chicken on the bed of vegetables.

4 Add the wine to the frying pan and bring to the boil. Pour the wine over the chicken and cover the casserole tightly. Cook in a preheated oven, 180°C/350°F/Gas Mark 4, for 50 minutes.

5 Add the olives to the chicken, mix lightly then pour on the cream. Re-cover the casserole and return to the oven for 10–20 minutes or until the chicken is very tender.

6 Adjust the seasoning and serve the pieces of chicken, surrounded by the vegetables and sauce, with pasta or tiny new potatoes. Sprinkle with parsley to garnish.

Step *2*

Step *3*

Step *5*

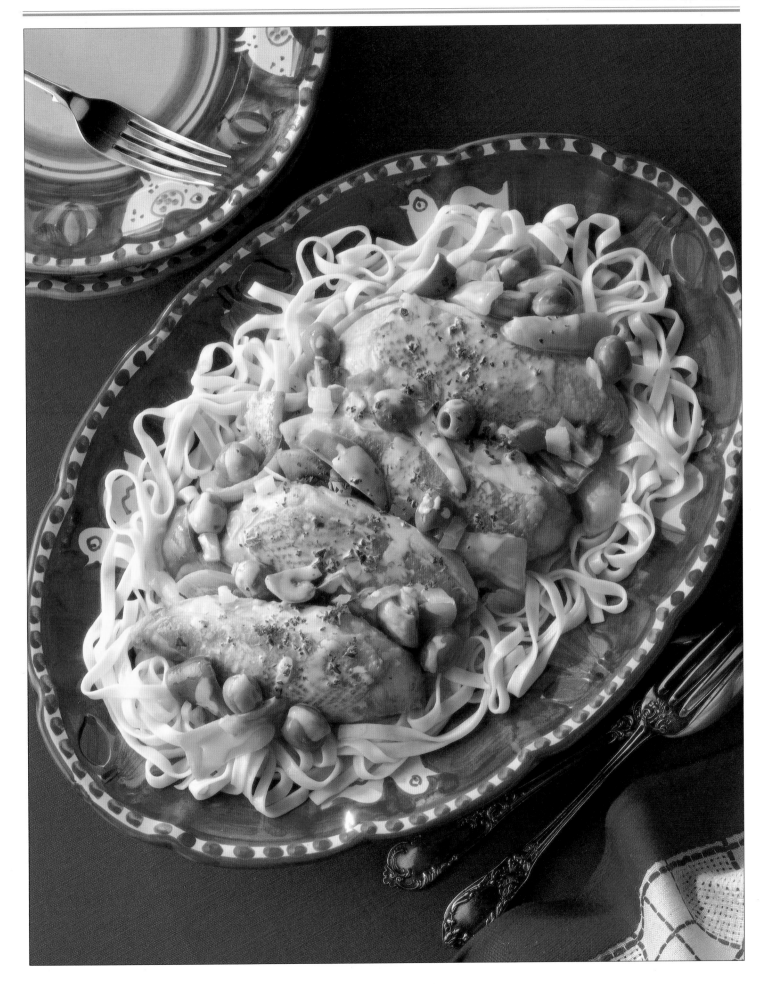

Chicken Scallops

Served in scallop shells, this makes a stylish presentation for a
dinner-party first course or a light lunch.

SERVES 4

INGREDIENTS

175 g/6 oz short-cut macaroni, or other
short pasta shapes
3 tbsp vegetable oil, plus extra for brushing
1 onion, chopped finely
3 rashers unsmoked collar or back bacon, rind
removed, chopped
125 g/4 oz button mushrooms,
sliced thinly or chopped
175 g/6 oz/¾ cup cooked chicken, diced
175 ml/6 fl oz/¾ cup crème fraîche
4 tbsp dry breadcrumbs
60 g/2 oz/½ cup mature (sharp) Cheddar, grated
salt and pepper
flat-leaf parsley sprigs, to garnish

1 Cook the pasta in a large pan of boiling salted water to which you have added 1 tablespoon of the oil. When the pasta is almost tender, drain in a colander, return to the pan and cover.

2 Heat the grill (broiler) to medium. Heat the remaining oil in a pan over medium heat and fry the onion until it is translucent. Add the chopped bacon and mushrooms and cook for a further 3–4 minutes, stirring once or twice.

3 Stir in the pasta, chicken and crème fraîche and season to taste with salt and pepper.

4 Brush four large scallop shells with oil. Spoon in the chicken mixture and smooth to make neat mounds.

5 Mix together the breadcrumbs and cheese, and sprinkle over the top of the shells. Press the topping lightly into the chicken mixture, and grill for 4–5 minutes, until golden brown and bubbling. Garnish with parsley, and serve hot.

Step *2*

Step *3*

Step *5*

Roman Chicken

This classic Roman dish makes an ideal light meal. It is equally good cold and could be taken on a picnic – serve with bread to mop up the juices.

SERVES 4

INGREDIENTS

4 tbsp olive oil
6 chicken pieces
2 garlic cloves, crushed with 1 tsp salt
1 large red onion, sliced
4 large mixed red, green and yellow (bell) peppers,
cored, deseeded and cut into strips
125 g/4 oz/⅔ cup pitted
green olives
½ quantity Tomato Sauce (page 44)
300 ml/½ pint/1¼ cups hot chicken stock
2 sprigs fresh marjoram
salt and pepper

1 Heat half the oil in a flameproof casserole and brown the chicken pieces on all sides. Remove the chicken pieces and set aside.

2 Add the remaining oil to the casserole and fry the garlic and onion until softened. Stir in the peppers, olives and tomato sauce.

3 Return the chicken to the casserole with the stock and marjoram. Cover the casserole and simmer for about 45 minutes until the chicken is tender. Season to taste with salt and pepper and serve with crusty bread.

Step *1*

Step *2*

Step *3*

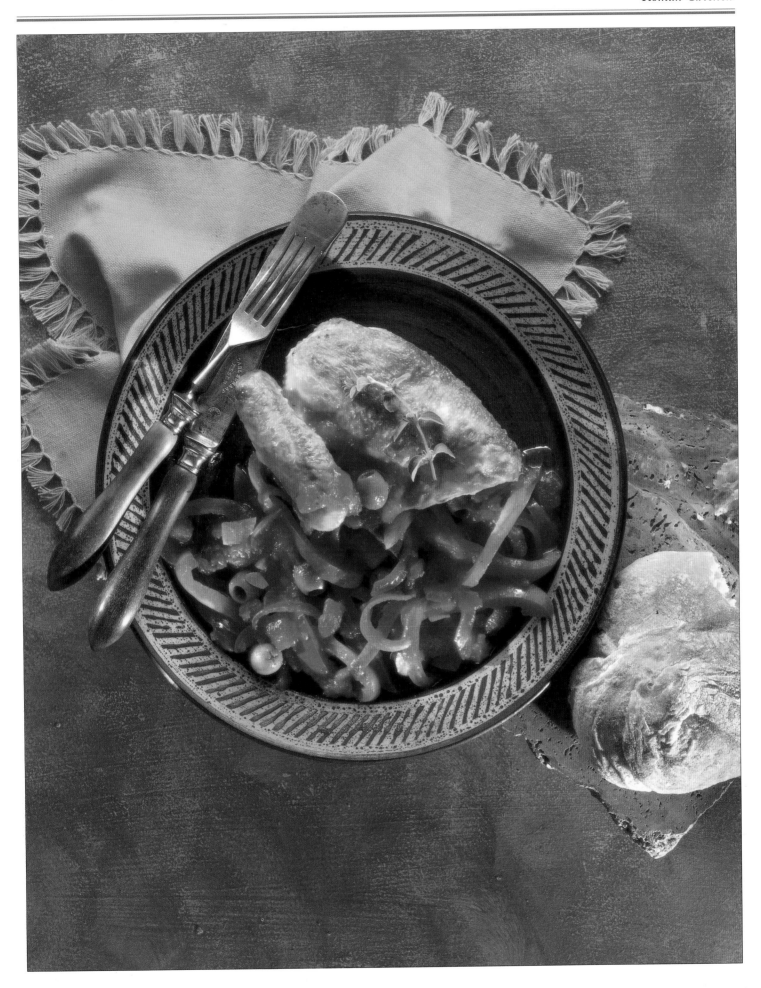

Pizzaiola Steak

This has a Neapolitan sauce, using the delicious red tomatoes so abundant in that area, but canned ones make an excellent alternative.

SERVES 4

INGREDIENTS

2 × 425 g/14 oz cans peeled tomatoes or
750 g/1½ lb fresh tomatoes
4 tbsp olive oil
2–3 garlic cloves, crushed
1 onion, chopped finely
1 tbsp tomato purée (paste)
1½ tsp chopped fresh marjoram or oregano
or ¾ tsp dried marjoram or oregano
4 thin sirloin or rump steaks
2 tbsp chopped fresh parsley
1 tsp sugar
salt and pepper
fresh herbs, to garnish (optional)
sauté potatoes, to serve

1 If using canned tomatoes, purée them in a food processor, then sieve to remove the seeds. If using fresh tomatoes, peel, remove the seeds and chop finely.

2 Heat half the oil in a pan and fry the garlic and onions very gently until soft – about 5 minutes.

3 Add the tomatoes, seasoning, tomato purée (paste) and chopped herbs to the pan. If using fresh tomatoes add 4 tablespoons water too, and then simmer very gently for 8–10 minutes, giving an occasional stir.

4 Meanwhile, trim the steaks if necessary and season with salt and pepper. Heat the remaining oil in a frying pan and fry the steaks quickly on both sides to seal, then continue until cooked to your liking – 2 minutes for rare, 3–4 minutes for medium, or 5 minutes for well done. Alternatively, cook the steaks under a hot grill (broiler) after brushing lightly with oil.

5 When the sauce has thickened a little, adjust the seasoning and stir in the chopped parsley and sugar.

6 Pour off the excess fat from the pan with the steaks and add the tomato sauce. Reheat gently and serve at once, with the sauce spooned over and around the steaks. Garnish with fresh herbs, if liked. Sauté potatoes make a good accompaniment with a green vegetable.

Step *4*

Step *5*

Step *6*

Beef in Barolo

Barolo is a famous wine from the Piedmont area of Italy. Its mellow flavour is the key to this dish, so don't stint on the quality of the wine.

SERVES 6

INGREDIENTS

4 tbsp oil
1 kg/2 lb piece boned rolled rib
of beef, or piece of silverside (round)
2 garlic cloves, crushed
4 shallots, sliced
1 tsp chopped fresh rosemary
1 tsp chopped fresh oregano
2 celery stalks, sliced
1 large carrot, diced
2 cloves
1 bottle Barolo wine
freshly grated nutmeg
salt and pepper

1 Heat the oil in a flameproof casserole and brown the meat all over. Remove the meat from the casserole.

2 Add the garlic, shallots, herbs, celery, carrot and cloves to the casserole and fry for 5 minutes.

3 Replace the meat on top of the vegetables. Pour in the wine. Cover the casserole and simmer gently for about 2 hours until tender. Remove the meat from the casserole, slice and keep warm.

4 Rub the contents of the pan through a sieve (strainer) or purée in a blender, adding a little hot beef stock if necessary. Season to taste with nutmeg, salt and pepper. Serve the meat with the sauce, accompanied by broccoli, carrots and new potatoes.

Step *1*

Step *3*

Step *4*

Beef Olives in Rich Gravy

Wafer-thin slices of tender beef with a rich garlic and bacon stuffing, flavoured with the tang of orange.

SERVES 4

INGREDIENTS

8 ready prepared beef olives
4 tbsp chopped fresh parsley
4 garlic cloves, chopped finely
125 g/4 oz smoked streaky bacon, rinded and chopped finely
grated rind of ½ small orange
2 tbsp olive oil
300 ml/½ pt/1¼ cups dry red wine
1 bay leaf
1 tsp sugar
60 g/2 oz pitted black olives, drained
salt and pepper

TO GARNISH

orange slices
chopped fresh parsley

1 Unroll the beef olives and flatten out as thinly as possible using a meat tenderizer or mallet. Trim the edges to neaten.

2 Mix together the parsley, garlic, bacon, orange rind and seasoning. Spread this mixture evenly over each beef olive.

3 Roll up each olive tightly, then secure with a cocktail stick (toothpick). Heat the oil in a frying pan (skillet) and fry the beef on all sides for 10 minutes.

4 Drain the beef olives, reserving the pan juices, and keep warm. Pour the wine into the juices, add the bay leaf, sugar and seasoning. Bring to the boil and boil rapidly for 5 minutes to reduce slightly.

5 Return the cooked beef to the pan along with the olives and heat through for a further 2 minutes. Discard the bay leaf and cocktail sticks (toothpicks).

6 Transfer the beef olives and gravy to a serving dish, and serve garnished with orange slices and parsley.

Step *1*

Step *3*

Step *4*

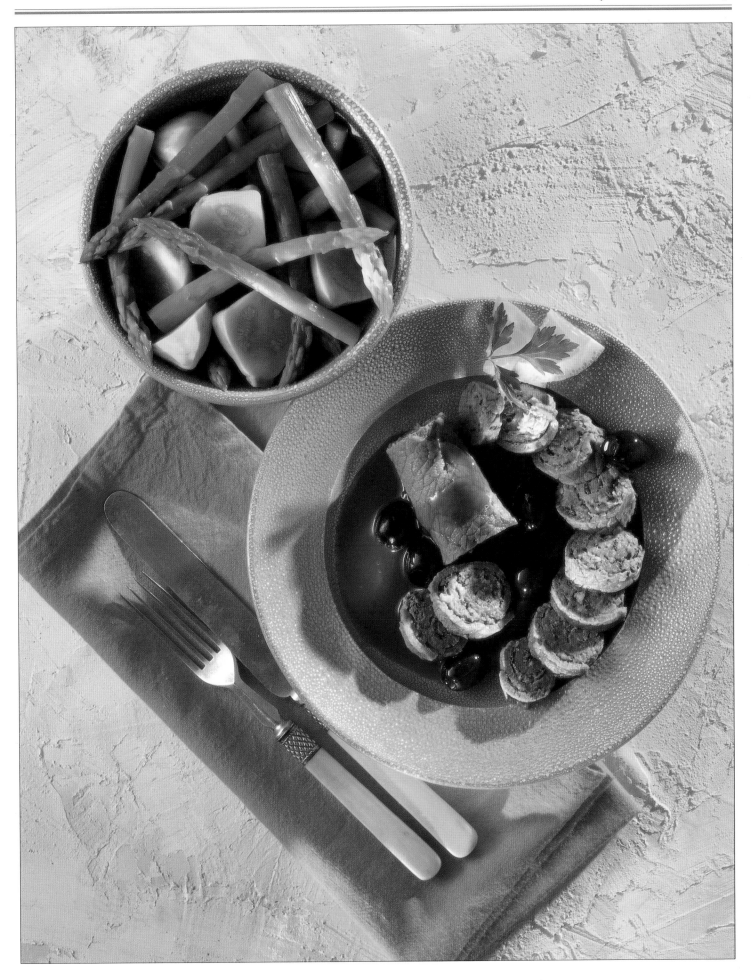

Saltimbocca

*Literally translated saltimbocca means 'jump in the mouth',
and this quick, tasty veal dish almost does that.*

SERVES 4

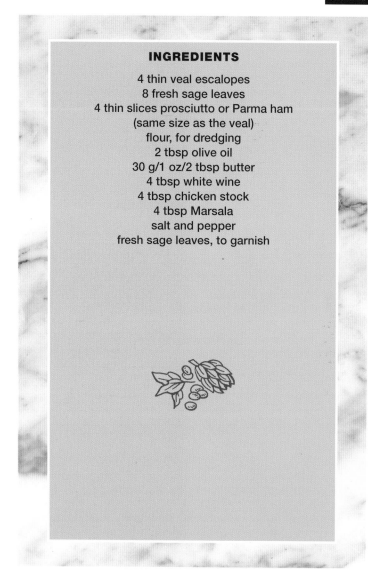

INGREDIENTS

4 thin veal escalopes
8 fresh sage leaves
4 thin slices prosciutto or Parma ham
(same size as the veal)
flour, for dredging
2 tbsp olive oil
30 g/1 oz/2 tbsp butter
4 tbsp white wine
4 tbsp chicken stock
4 tbsp Marsala
salt and pepper
fresh sage leaves, to garnish

1 Either leave the escalopes as they are or cut in half. Place the pieces of veal on a sheet of clingfilm (plastic wrap) or baking parchment, keeping well apart, and cover with another piece.

2 Using a meat mallet or rolling pin beat the escalopes gently until at least double in size and very thin.

3 Lightly season the escalopes with salt and pepper and lay two fresh sage leaves on the large slices, or one on each of the smaller slices. Then lay the prosciutto slices evenly over the escalopes to cover the sage and fit the size of the veal almost exactly.

4 Secure the prosciutto to the veal with wooden cocktail sticks. If preferred, the large slices can be folded in half first. Dredge lightly with a little flour.

5 Heat the olive oil and butter in a large frying pan (skillet) and fry the escalopes until golden brown each side and just cooked through – about 4 minutes for single slices or 5–6 minutes for double ones. Take care not to overcook. Remove to a serving dish and keep warm.

6 Add the wine, stock and Marsala to the pan and bring to the boil, stirring well to loosen all the sediment from the pan. Boil until reduced by almost half. Adjust the seasoning and quickly pour over the saltimbocca. Serve at once, garnished with fresh sage leaves.

Step *2*

Step *3*

Step *5*

Vitello Tonnato

Veal dishes are the speciality of Lombardy, with this dish being one of the more sophisticated. Serve cold with seasonal salads.

SERVES 4

INGREDIENTS

750 g/1½ lb boned leg of veal, rolled
2 bay leaves
10 black peppercorns
2–3 cloves
½ tsp salt
2 carrots, sliced
1 onion, sliced
2 celery stalks, sliced
about 750 ml/1¼ pints/3 cups
stock or water
150 ml/¼ pint/⅔ cup dry white wine
(optional)
90 g/3 oz canned tuna fish, well drained
50 g (1½ oz) can anchovy fillets, drained
150 ml/¼ pint/⅔ cup olive oil
2 tsp bottled capers, drained
2 egg yolks
1 tbsp lemon juice
salt and pepper

TO GARNISH

capers
lemon wedges
fresh herbs

1 Put the veal in a saucepan with the bay leaves, peppercorns, cloves, salt and vegetables. Add sufficient stock or water and the wine (if using) to barely cover the veal. Bring to the boil, remove any scum from the surface, then cover the pan and simmer gently for an hour or so until tender. Leave in the water until cold, then drain thoroughly. If time allows, chill the veal to make it easier to carve.

2 For the tuna sauce: thoroughly mash the tuna with four anchovy fillets, 1 tablespoon oil and the capers. Add the egg yolks and press through a sieve (strainer) or purée in a food processor or liquidizer until smooth.

3 Stir in the lemon juice then gradually whisk in the rest of the oil a few drops at a time until the sauce is smooth and has the consistency of thick cream. Season with salt and pepper to taste.

4 Slice the veal thinly and arrange on a platter in overlapping slices. Spoon the sauce over the veal to cover. Then cover the dish and chill overnight.

5 Before serving, uncover the veal carefully. Arrange the remaining anchovy fillets and the capers in a decorative pattern on top, and garnish with lemon wedges and herbs.

Step *1*

Step *3*

Step *4*

Liver with Wine Sauce

Liver is popular in Italy and is served in many ways. Tender calf's liver is the best to use for this recipe, but you could use lamb's liver.

SERVES 4

INGREDIENTS

4 slices calf's liver or 8 slices lamb's liver,
about 500 g/1 lb
flour, for coating
1 tbsp olive oil
30 g/1 oz/2 tbsp butter
1 garlic clove, crushed
125 g/4 oz lean bacon rashers, rinded and cut into
narrow strips
1 onion, chopped
1 celery stalk, sliced thinly
150 ml/½ pint/⅔ cup red wine
150 ml/½ pint/⅔ cup beef stock
good pinch of ground allspice
1 tsp Worcestershire sauce
1 tsp chopped fresh sage or ½ tsp
dried sage
3–4 tomatoes, peeled, quartered and deseeded
salt and pepper
fresh sage leaves, to garnish
new potatoes or sauté potatoes, to serve

1 Wipe the liver, season with salt and pepper and coat lightly in flour, shaking off the surplus.

2 Heat the oil and butter in a pan and fry the liver until well sealed on both sides and just cooked through – take care not to overcook. Remove the liver from the pan, cover and keep warm, but do not allow to dry out.

3 Add the bacon to the fat left in the pan, with the onion and celery. Fry gently until soft.

4 Add the wine, stock, allspice, Worcestershire sauce and seasonings. Bring to the boil and simmer for 3–4 minutes.

5 Cut each tomato segment in half. Add to the sauce and continue to cook for a couple of minutes.

6 Serve the liver on a little of the sauce, with the remainder spooned over. Garnish with fresh sage leaves and serve with tiny new potatoes or sauté potatoes.

Step *1*

Step *2*

Step *4*

Pot Roasted Leg of Lamb

*This dish from the Abruzzi uses a slow cooking method which ensures
that the meat absorbs the flavourings and becomes very tender.*

SERVES 4

INGREDIENTS

1.75 kg/3½ lb leg of lamb
3–4 sprigs fresh rosemary
125 g/4 oz streaky bacon rashers
4 tbsp olive oil
2–3 garlic cloves, crushed
2 onions, sliced
2 carrots, sliced
2 celery stalks, sliced
300 ml/½ pint/1¼ cups dry white wine
1 tbsp tomato purée (paste)
300 ml/½ pint/1¼ cups stock
350 g/12 oz tomatoes, peeled, quartered
and deseeded
1 tbsp chopped fresh parsley
1 tbsp chopped fresh oregano or marjoram
salt and pepper
fresh rosemary sprigs, to garnish

1 Wipe the joint of lamb all over, trimming off any excess fat, then season well with salt and pepper, rubbing well in. Lay the sprigs of rosemary over the lamb, cover evenly with the bacon rashers and tie in place with fine string.

2 Heat the oil in a frying pan (skillet) and fry the lamb until browned all over, turning several times – about 10 minutes. Remove from the pan.

3 Transfer the oil from the frying pan (skillet) to a large fireproof casserole and fry the garlic and onion together for 3–4 minutes until beginning to soften. Add the carrots and celery, and continue to cook for a few minutes longer.

4 Lay the lamb on top of the vegetables and press well to partly submerge. Pour the wine over the lamb, add the tomato purée (paste) and simmer for 3–4 minutes. Add the stock, tomatoes and herbs and seasoning and bring back to the boil for a further 3–4 minutes.

5 Cover the casserole tightly and cook in a moderate oven, 180°C/350°F/Gas Mark 4, for 2–2½ hours until very tender.

6 Remove the lamb from the casserole and if liked, take off the bacon and herbs along with the string. Keep warm. Strain the juices, skimming off any excess fat, and serve in a jug. The vegetables may be put around the joint or in a serving dish. Garnish with fresh sprigs of rosemary.

Step *1*

Step *4*

Step *6*

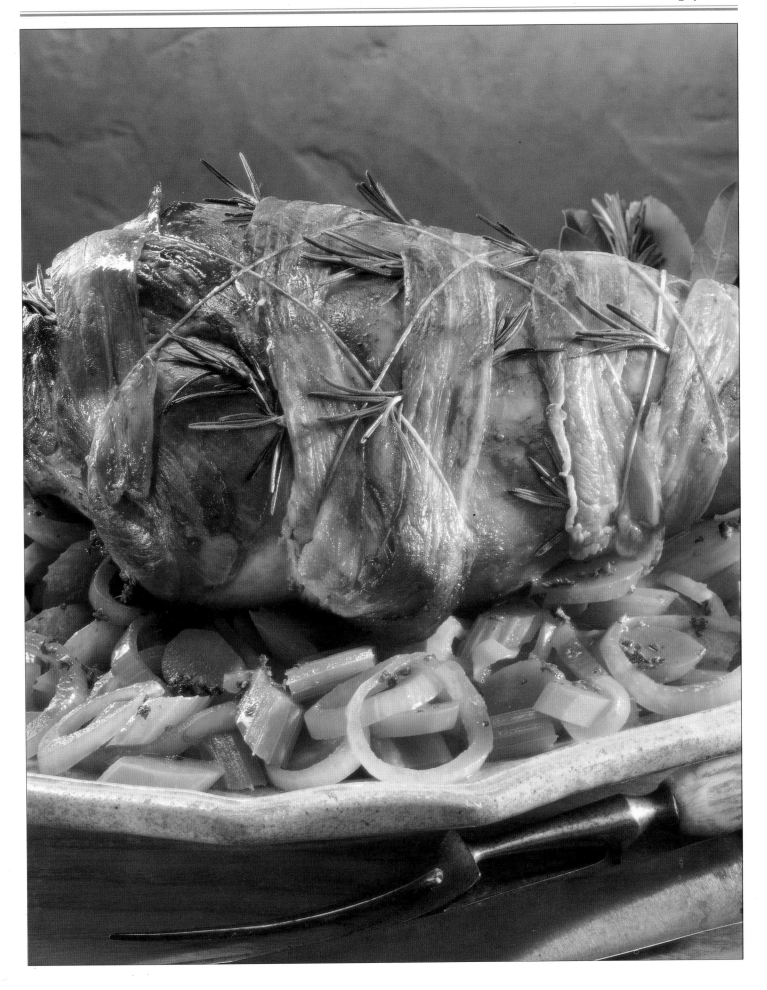

Lamb with Olives

This is a very simple dish, and the chilli gives it a kick. It is quick to prepare and makes an ideal supper dish.

SERVES 4

INGREDIENTS

1.25 kg/2½ lb boned leg of lamb
90 ml/3 fl oz/⅓ cup olive oil
2 garlic cloves, crushed
1 onion, sliced
1 small red chilli, cored, deseeded
and chopped finely
175 ml/6 fl oz/¾ cup dry white wine
175 g/6 oz/1 cup pitted black olives
salt
chopped fresh parsley, to garnish

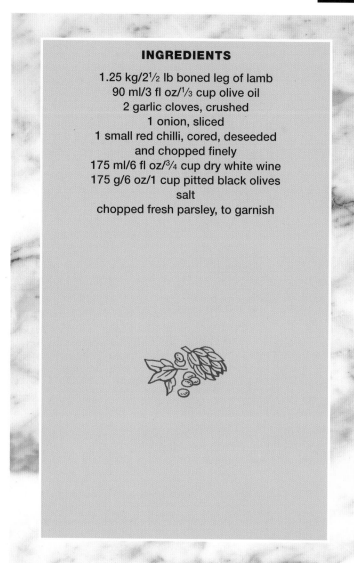

1 Cut the lamb into 2.5 cm/ 1 inch cubes.

2 Heat the oil in a frying pan (skillet) and fry the garlic, onion and chilli for 5 minutes.

3 Add the wine and meat and cook for a further 5 minutes.

4 Stir in the olives, then transfer the mixture to a casserole. Place in a preheated oven, 180°C/350°F/ Gas Mark 4, and cook for about 1 hour 20 minutes until the meat is tender. Season to taste with salt, and serve garnished with chopped fresh parsley.

Step *1*

Step *3*

Step *4*

Pork Chops with Sage

*The fresh taste of sage is the perfect ingredient
to counteract the richness of pork.*

INGREDIENTS

2 tbsp flour
1 tbsp chopped fresh sage or 1 tsp dried
4 lean boneless pork chops, trimmed of excess fat
2 tbsp olive oil
15 g/½ oz/1 tbsp butter
2 red onions, sliced into rings
1 tbsp lemon juice
2 tsp caster (superfine) sugar
4 plum tomatoes, quartered
salt and pepper

1 Mix the flour, sage and salt and pepper on a plate. Lightly dust the pork chops on both sides with the seasoned flour.

2 Heat the oil and butter in a frying pan (skillet), add the chops and cook them for 6–7 minutes on each side until cooked through.

3 Drain the chops, reserving the pan juices, and keep warm.

4 Toss the onion in the lemon juice and fry along with the sugar and tomatoes for 5 minutes until tender.

5 Serve the pork accompanied with the tomato and onion mixture and a green salad.

Step *1*

Step *2*

Step *4*

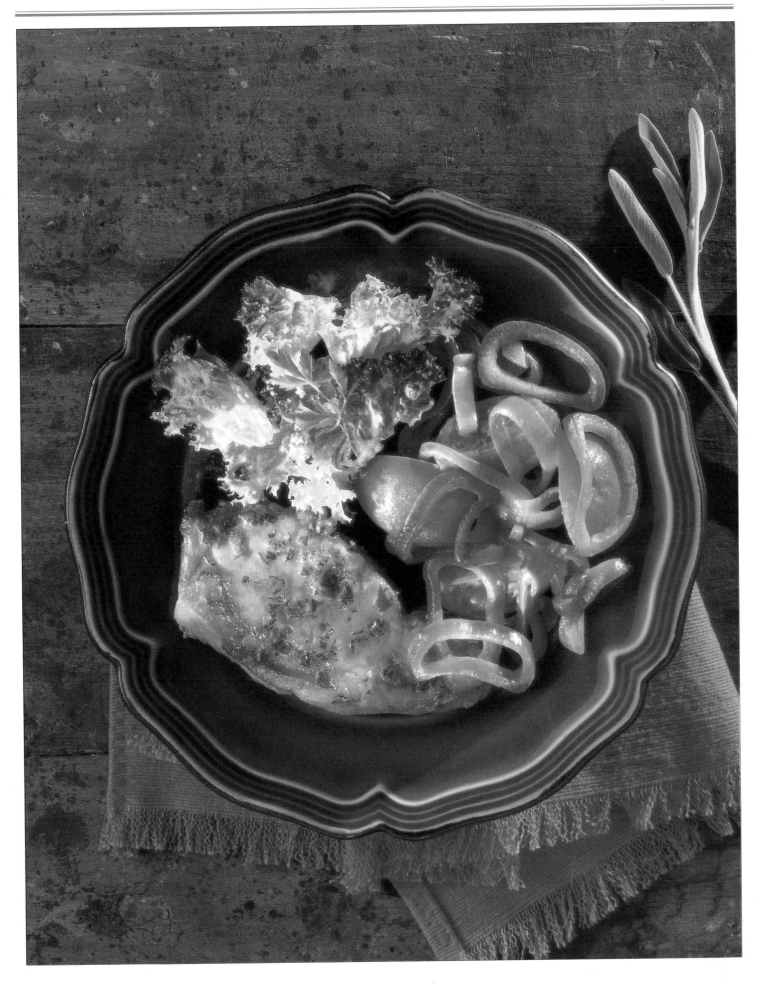

Pork Fillet Stuffed with Prosciutto

*A sophisticated roast with Mediterranean flavours
is ideal served with a pungent olive paste.*

SERVES 4

INGREDIENTS

500 g/1 lb piece of lean pork fillet
small bunch fresh of basil leaves, washed
2 tbsp freshly grated Parmesan
2 tbsp sun-dried tomato paste
6 thin slices prosciutto or Parma ham
1 tbsp olive oil
salt and pepper

OLIVE PASTE

125 g/4 oz/²⁄₃ cup pitted black olives
4 tbsp olive oil
2 garlic cloves, peeled

1 Trim away excess fat and membrane from the pork fillet. Slice the pork lengthways down the middle, taking care not to cut all the way through.

2 Open out the pork and season the inside. Lay the basil leaves down the centre. Mix the cheese and sun-dried tomato paste and spread on top of the basil.

3 Press the pork back together. Wrap the ham around the pork, overlapping, to cover. Place on a rack in a roasting tin, seamside down, and brush with olive oil. Bake in a preheated oven, 190°C/375°F/Gas Mark 5, for 30–40 minutes depending on thickness until cooked through. Allow to stand for 10 minutes.

4 For the olive paste, place all the ingredients in a blender or food processor and blend until smooth. Alternatively, for a coarser paste, finely chop the olives and garlic and mix with the oil.

5 Drain the cooked pork and slice thinly to serve, accompanied with the olive paste and a salad.

Step *1*

Step *3*

Step *4*

RICE, POLENTA & GNOCCHI

Rice dishes are particularly popular in the north of Italy where a fair amount is consumed in risottos. Milanese and other risottos are made with short-grain Italian rice, the best of which is Arborio, but remember that this type of rice should be rinsed before using.
An Italian risotto is far moister than a pilau or other savoury rice dish, but it should not be soggy or sticky. Gnocchi are made with maize flour, cornmeal (polenta), potatoes or semolina, often combined with spinach or some sort of cheese. Gnocchi resemble dumplings and are either poached or baked, and served with a cheese sauce.
Polenta is made with either cornmeal or polenta flour and can be served either as a soft porridge or a firmer cake which is then fried until crisp. The traditional method of making polenta involved lengthy and laborious stirring, but there is now an excellent polenta mix available which cuts the time to five minutes!

Potato Gnocchi with Garlic & Herb Sauce

These little potato dumplings are a traditional Italian appetizer but, served with a salad and bread, they make a substantial meal.

SERVES 4–6

INGREDIENTS

1 kg/2 lb old potatoes, cut into
1 cm/½ inch pieces
60 g/2 oz/¼ cup butter or margarine
1 egg, beaten
300 g/10 oz/2½ cups plain (all-purpose) flour
salt

SAUCE

120 ml/4 fl oz/½ cup olive oil
2 garlic cloves, very finely chopped
1 tbsp chopped fresh oregano
1 tbsp chopped fresh basil
salt and pepper

TO SERVE

freshly grated Parmesan (optional)
mixed salad (greens)
warm ciabatta

1 Cook the potatoes in boiling salted water for about 10 minutes or until tender. Drain well.

2 Press the hot potatoes through a sieve (strainer) into a large bowl. Add 1 teaspoon of salt, the butter or margarine, egg and 150 g/5 oz/1¼ cups of the flour. Mix well to bind together.

3 Turn on to a lightly floured surface and knead, gradually adding the remaining flour, until a smooth, soft, slightly sticky dough is formed.

4 Flour the hands and roll the dough into 2 cm/¾ inch thick rolls. Cut into 1 cm/½ inch pieces. Press the top of each one with the floured prongs of a fork and spread out on a floured tea towel (dish cloth).

5 Bring a large saucepan of salted water to a simmer. Add the gnocchi and cook in batches for 2–3 minutes until they rise to the surface.

6 Remove with a perforated spoon and put in a warmed, greased serving dish. Cover and keep warm.

7 To make the sauce, put the oil, garlic and seasoning in a saucepan and cook gently, stirring, for 3–4 minutes until the garlic is golden. Remove from the heat and stir in the herbs. Pour over the gnocchi and serve immediately, sprinkled with Parmesan, if liked, and accompanied by salad and warm ciabatta.

Step *2*

Step *3*

Step *4*

Gnocchi Romana

This is a traditional recipe from Piedmont. For a less rich version, omit the eggs. Serve as a starter, or a main meal with a crisp salad.

SERVES 4

INGREDIENTS

750 ml/1¼ pints/3 cups milk
¼ tsp freshly grated nutmeg
90 g/3 oz/6 tbsp butter, plus extra for greasing
250 g/8 oz/1⅓ cups semolina
125 g/4 oz/1 cup Parmesan, grated
2 eggs, beaten
60 g/2 oz/½ cup Gruyère, grated
salt and pepper
basil sprigs, to garnish

1 Bring the milk to the boil, remove from the heat and stir in the seasoning, nutmeg and 30 g/1 oz/2 tablespoons of butter. Gradually add the semolina, whisking to prevent lumps forming, and return to a low heat. Simmer gently for about 10 minutes, stirring constantly, until very thick.

2 Beat 60 g/2 oz/½ cup of Parmesan into the semolina, followed by the eggs. Continue beating until the mixture is quite smooth.

3 Spread out the semolina mixture in an even layer on a sheet of baking parchment or in a large oiled baking tin (pan), smoothing the surface with a wet spatula – it should be about 1 cm/½ inch thick. Leave until cold, then chill for about an hour until firm.

4 Cut the gnocchi into circles about 4 cm/1½ inches in diameter, using a plain greased pastry cutter.

5 Thoroughly grease a shallow ovenproof dish, or four individual dishes. Lay the gnocchi trimmings in the base of the dish and cover with overlapping circles of gnocchi. Melt the remaining butter and drizzle all over the gnocchi, then sprinkle first with the remaining Parmesan and then with the Gruyère.

6 Cook the gnocchi in a preheated oven, 200°C/400°F/Gas Mark 4, for 25–30 minutes until the top is crisp and golden brown.

Step *2*

Step *3*

Step *4*

Spinach and Ricotta Gnocchi

Try not to handle the mixture too much when making gnocchi,
as this will make the dough a little heavy.

SERVES 4

INGREDIENTS:

1 kg/2 lb spinach
350 g/12 oz/1½ cups Ricotta
125 g/4 oz/1 cup Pecorino, grated
3 eggs, beaten
¼ tsp freshly grated nutmeg
plain (all-purpose) flour
125 g/4 oz/½ cup unsalted butter
25 g/1 oz/¼ cup pine kernels (nuts)
50 g/2 oz/⅓ cup raisins
salt and pepper

1 Wash and drain the spinach well and cook in a covered saucepan without any extra liquid until softened, about 8 minutes. Place in a colander and press well to remove as much juice as possible. Either rub through a sieve (strainer) or purée in a blender.

2 Combine the spinach purée with the Ricotta, half the Pecorino, the eggs, nutmeg and seasoning to taste, mixing lightly but thoroughly. Work in enough flour, lightly and quickly, to make the mixture easy to handle.

3 Shape the dough quickly into small lozenge shapes, and dust lightly with flour.

4 Add a dash of oil to a large pan of salted water and bring to the boil. Add the gnocchi carefully and boil for about 2 minutes until they float on the top. Use a perforated spoon and transfer to a buttered ovenproof dish. Keep warm.

5 Melt the butter in a frying pan (skillet). Add the pine kernels (nuts) and raisins and fry until the nuts start to brown slightly, but do not allow the butter to burn. Pour the mixture over the gnocchi and serve sprinkled with the remaining Pecorino.

Step *2*

Step *3*

Step *5*

Polenta

*Polenta is prepared and served in a variety of ways and can be served
hot or cold, sweet or savoury.*

SERVES 4

INGREDIENTS

1.5 litres/2⅓ pints/7 cups water
1½ tsp salt
300 g/10 oz/2 cups polenta or cornmeal flour
2 beaten eggs (optional)
125 g/4 oz/2 cups fresh fine white
breadcrumbs (optional)
vegetable oil, for frying and oiling
2 quantities Basic Tomato Sauce (page 13)

MUSHROOM SAUCE

3 tbsp olive oil
250 g/8 oz mushrooms, sliced
2 garlic cloves, crushed
150 ml/¼ pint/⅔ cup dry white wine
4 tbsp double (heavy) cream
2 tbsp chopped fresh mixed herbs
salt and pepper

1 Bring the water and salt to the boil in a large pan and gradually sprinkle in the polenta or cornmeal flour, stirring all the time to prevent lumps forming.

2 Simmer the mixture very gently, stirring frequently, until the polenta becomes very thick and starts to draw away from the sides of the pan, about 30–35 minutes. It is likely to splatter, in which case partially cover the pan with a lid.

3 Thoroughly oil a shallow tin, about 28 × 18 cm/ 11 × 7 inches, and spoon in the polenta. Spread out evenly, using a wet spatula. Allow to cool, then leave to stand for a few hours at room temperature, if possible.

4 Cut the polenta into 30–36 squares. Heat the oil in a frying pan (skillet) and fry the pieces until golden brown all over, turning several times – about 5 minutes. Alternatively, dip each piece of polenta in beaten egg and coat in breadcrumbs before frying in the hot oil.

5 To make the mushroom sauce: heat the oil in a pan and fry the mushrooms with the crushed garlic for 3–4 minutes. Add the wine, season well and simmer for 5 minutes. Add the cream and chopped herbs and simmer for another minute or so.

6 Serve the polenta with either the tomato sauce or mushroom sauce.

Step *2*

Step *3*

Step *4*

Lazy Polenta with Rabbit Stew

*Polenta can be served fresh, as in this dish, or it can be cooled,
then sliced and grilled (broiled).*

SERVES 4

INGREDIENTS

300 g/10 oz/2 cups polenta or cornmeal
1 tbsp coarse sea salt
1.25 litres/2 pints/5 cups water
4 tbsp olive oil
2 kg/4 lb rabbit joints (pieces)
3 garlic cloves, peeled
3 shallots, sliced
150 ml/¼ pint/⅔ cup red wine
1 carrot, sliced
1 celery stalk, sliced
2 bay leaves
1 sprig rosemary
3 tomatoes, peeled and diced
90 g/3 oz/½ cup pitted black olives
salt and pepper

1 Butter a large ovenproof dish. Mix the polenta, salt and water in a large saucepan, whisking well to prevent lumps forming. Bring to the boil and boil for 10 minutes, stirring vigorously. Turn into the buttered dish and bake in a preheated oven, 190°C/375°F/Gas Mark 5, for 40 minutes.

2 Meanwhile, heat the oil in a large saucepan and add the rabbit pieces, garlic and shallots. Fry for 10 minutes until browned.

3 Stir in the wine and cook for a further 5 minutes.

4 Add the carrot, celery, bay leaves, rosemary, tomatoes, olives and 300 ml/½ pint/1¼ cups water. Cover the pan and simmer for about 45 minutes until the rabbit is tender. Season to taste.

5 To serve, spoon or cut a portion of polenta and place on each serving plate. Top with a ladleful of stew.

Step *2*

Step *3*

Step *4*

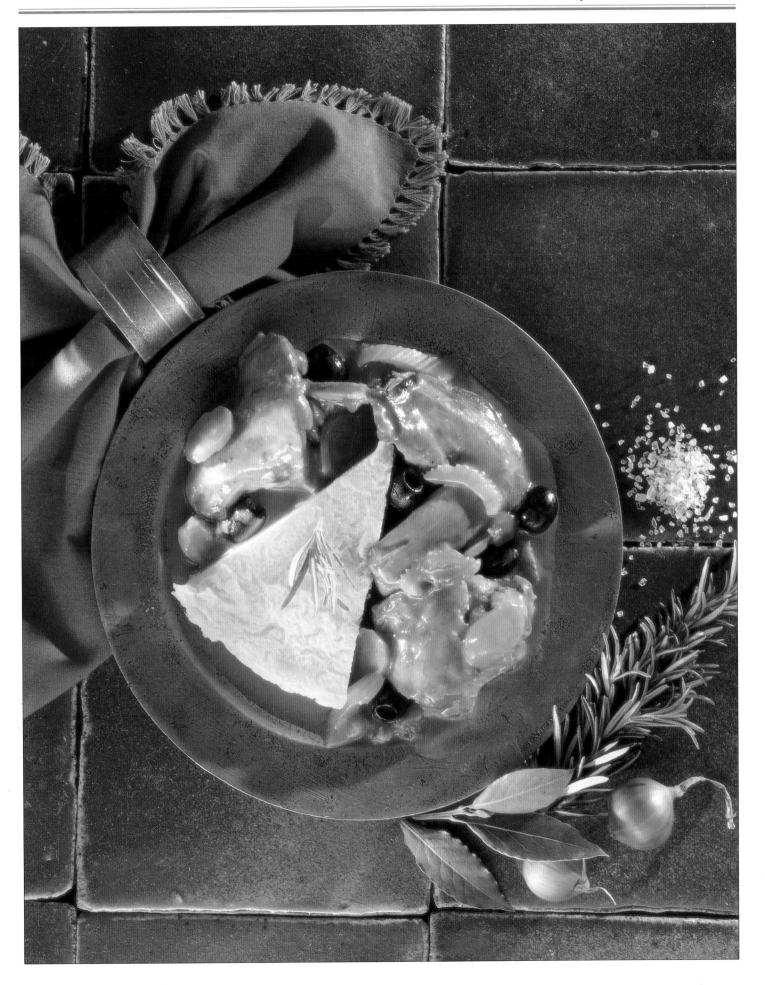

Milanese Risotto

*Italian rice is a round, short-grained variety with a nutty flavour, which
is essential for a good risotto. Arborio is a good one to use.*

SERVES 4

INGREDIENTS

2 good pinches of saffron threads
1 large onion, chopped finely
1–2 garlic cloves, crushed
90 g/3 oz/6 tbsp butter
350 g/12 oz/1⅔ cups Arborio or other
short-grain Italian rice
150 ml/¼ pint/⅔ cup dry white wine
1.25 litres/2 pints/5 cups boiling stock
(chicken, beef or vegetable)
90 g/3 oz/¾ cup Parmesan, grated
salt and pepper

1 Put the saffron in a small bowl, cover with 3–4 tablespoons boiling water and leave to soak while cooking the risotto.

2 Fry the onion and garlic in 60 g/2 oz of the butter until soft but not coloured, then add the rice and continue to cook for a few minutes until all the grains are coated in oil and beginning to colour lightly.

3 Add the wine to the rice and simmer gently, stirring from time to time until it is all absorbed.

4 Add the boiling stock a little at a time, about 150 ml/¼ pint/⅔ cup, cooking until the liquid is fully absorbed before adding more, and stirring frequently.

5 When all the stock is absorbed the rice should be tender but not soft and soggy. Add the saffron liquid, Parmesan, remaining butter and plenty of seasoning. Simmer for a minute or so until piping hot and thoroughly mixed.

6 Cover the pan tightly and leave to stand for 5 minutes off the heat. Give a good stir and serve at once.

Step *1*

Step *2*

Step *5*

Rice and Peas

If you can get fresh peas (and willing helpers to shell them), do use them:
you will need 1 kg/2 lb. Add to the pan with the stock.

SERVES 4

INGREDIENTS

1 tbsp olive oil
60 g/2 oz/¼ cup butter
60 g/2 oz/¼ cup pancetta
(Italian unsmoked bacon), chopped
1 small onion, chopped
1.4 litres/2½ pints/6¼ cups hot chicken stock
200 g/7 oz/1 cup risotto rice
3 tbsp chopped fresh parsley
250 g/8 oz/1¼ cups frozen or
canned petits pois
60 g/2 oz/½ cup Parmesan, grated
pepper

1 Heat the oil with half the butter. Add the pancetta (Italian unsmoked bacon) and onion, and fry for 5 minutes. Add the stock (and fresh peas if using) and bring to the boil.

2 Stir in the rice and season to taste with pepper. Cook until the rice is tender, about 20–30 minutes, stirring occasionally.

3 Add the parsley and frozen or canned petits pois and cook for 8 minutes until the peas are thoroughly heated.

4 Stir in the remaining butter and the Parmesan. Serve immediately, with freshly ground black pepper.

Step *1*

Step *3*

Step *4*

PIZZAS

There is little to beat the irresistible aroma and taste of a freshly made pizza cooked in a wood-fired brick oven. However, a homemade dough base and a freshly made tomato sauce will give you the closest thing possible to an authentic Italian pizza.

Pizzas can have every imaginable type of topping. There are endless varieties of salamis and cured meats, hams and sausages which all make excellent toppings. Canned or fresh fish or seafood are also good. The most popular fish for pizzas are anchovies and you either love them or hate them. If you find them too salty, soak them in a little milk before using.

Vegetables of all kinds make the most attractive and tempting pizza toppings. Choose the best quality vegetables and herbs for maximum flavour. A variety of antipasti are sold in jars of olive oil, such as artichoke hearts, sun-dried tomatoes, sliced (bell) peppers and mushrooms. These make the most delicious and convenient toppings, and you can use the oil from the jar to drizzle over the pizza before baking to keep it moist.

Bread Dough Base

Traditionally, pizza bases are made from bread dough; this recipe will give you a base similar to an Italian pizza.

MAKES ONE 25 CM/10 INCH PIZZA

INGREDIENTS

15 g/½ oz fresh yeast or 1 tsp dried
or easy-blend yeast
90 ml/3½ fl oz/6 tbsp tepid water
½ tsp sugar
1 tbsp olive oil
175 g/6 oz plain flour
1 tsp salt

1 Combine the fresh yeast with the water and sugar in a bowl. If using dried yeast, sprinkle it over the surface of the water and whisk in until dissolved.

2 Leave the mixture to rest in a warm place for 10–15 minutes until frothy on the surface. Stir in the olive oil.

3 Sift the flour and salt into a large bowl. If using easy-blend yeast, stir it in at this point. Make a well in the centre and pour in the yeast liquid, or water and oil (without the sugar for easy-blend yeast).

4 Using either floured hands or a wooden spoon, mix together to form a dough. Turn out on to a floured work surface and knead for about 5 minutes until smooth and elastic.

5 Place in a large greased plastic bag and leave in a warm place for about 1 hour or until doubled in size. Airing cupboards are often the best places for this, as the temperature remains constant.

6 Turn out on to a lightly floured work surface and 'knock back' by punching the dough. This releases any air bubbles which would make the pizza uneven. Knead 4 or 5 times. The dough is now ready to use.

Step *3*

Step *4*

Step *6*

Scone (Biscuit) Base

This is a quick and easy alternative to the bread dough base. If you do not have time to wait for bread dough to rise, a scone (biscuit) base is ideal.

MAKES ONE 25 CM/10 INCH BASE

INGREDIENTS

175 g/6 oz self-raising flour
½ tsp salt
30 g/1 oz butter
120 ml/4 fl oz/½ cup milk

1 Sift the flour and salt into a bowl.

2 Rub in the butter with your fingertips until it resembles fine breadcrumbs.

3 Make a well in the centre of the flour and butter mixture and pour in nearly all the milk at once. Mix in quickly with a knife. Add the remaining milk only if necessary to mix to a soft dough.

4 Turn the dough out on to a floured work surface and knead by turning and pressing with the heel of your hand 3 or 4 times.

5 Either roll out or press the dough into a 25 cm/ 10 inch circle on a lightly greased baking sheet (cookie sheet) or pizza pan. Push up the edge slightly all round to form a ridge and use immediately.

Step 2

Step 4

Step 5

Potato Base

This is an unusual pizza base made from mashed potatoes and flour and is a great way to use up any leftover boiled potatoes.

MAKES ONE 25 CM/10 IN BASE

INGREDIENTS

250 g/8 oz boiled potatoes
g/2 oz/¼ cup butter or margarine
'5 g/4 oz/1 cup self-raising flour
½ tsp salt

1 If the potatoes are hot, mash them, then stir in the butter until it has melted and is distributed evenly throughout the potatoes. Leave to cool.

2 Sift the flour and salt together and stir into the mashed potato to form a soft dough.

3 If the potatoes are cold, mash them without adding the butter. Sift the flour and salt into a bowl. Rub in the butter with your fingertips until the mixture resembles fine breadcrumbs, then stir the flour and butter mixture into the mashed potatoes to form a soft dough.

4 Either roll out or press the dough into a 25 cm/ 10 inch circle on a lightly greased baking sheet (cookie sheet) or pizza pan, pushing up the edge slightly all round to form a ridge before adding the topping. This base is tricky to lift before it is cooked, so you will find it easier to handle if you roll it out directly on to the baking sheet (cookie sheet).

5 If the base is not required for cooking immediately, you can cover it with clingfilm (plastic wrap) and chill it for up to 2 hours.

Step *2*

Step *3*

Step *4*

Tomato Sauce

Using canned chopped tomatoes for this dish saves time, and they are preferable to plum tomatoes which tend to be on the watery side.

MAKES 175 ML/6 FL OZ

INGREDIENTS

1 small onion, chopped
1 garlic clove, crushed
1 tbsp olive oil
200 g/7 oz can chopped tomatoes
2 tsp tomato purée (paste)
½ tsp sugar
½ tsp dried oregano
1 bay leaf
salt and pepper

1 Fry the onion and garlic gently in the oil for 5 minutes until softened but not browned.

2 Add the tomatoes, tomato purée (paste), sugar, oregano, bay leaf and seasoning. Stir well.

3 Bring to the boil, cover and simmer gently for 20 minutes, stirring occasionally, until you have a thickish sauce.

4 Remove the bay leaf and adjust the seasoning to taste. Leave to cool completely before using. This sauce keeps well in a screw-top jar in the refrigerator for up to a week.

Step *1*

Step *2*

Step *4*

Special Tomato Sauce

This sauce is made with fresh tomatoes. Use the plum variety whenever available and always choose the reddest ones for the best flavour.

MAKES 180 ML/6 FL OZ

INGREDIENTS

1 small onion, chopped
1 small red (bell) pepper, chopped
1 garlic clove, crushed
2 tbsp olive oil
250 g/8 oz tomatoes
1 tbsp tomato purée (paste)
1 tsp soft brown sugar
2 tsp chopped fresh basil
½ tsp dried oregano
1 bay leaf
salt and pepper

1 Fry the onion, (bell) pepper and garlic gently in the oil for 5 minutes until softened but not browned.

2 Cut a cross in the base of each tomato and place them in a bowl. Pour on boiling water and leave for about 45 seconds. Drain, and then plunge in cold water. The skins will slide off easily.

3 Chop the tomatoes, discarding any hard cores. Add to the onion mix with the tomato purée (paste), sugar, herbs and seasoning. Stir well. Bring to the boil, cover and simmer gently for 30 minutes, stirring occasionally, until you have a thickish sauce.

4 Remove the bay leaf and adjust the seasoning to taste. Leave to cool completely before using.

5 This sauce will keep well in a screw-top jar in the refrigerator for up to a week.

Step *1*

Step *2*

Step *3*

Four Seasons

This is a traditional pizza on which the toppings are divided into four sections, each of which is supposed to depict a season of the year.

SERVES 2-4

INGREDIENTS

Bread Dough Base (page 186)
Special Tomato Sauce (page 194)
30 g/1 oz chorizo sausage, sliced thinly
30 g/1 oz button mushrooms, wiped
and sliced thinly
45 g/1½ oz artichoke hearts, sliced thinly
30 g/1 oz Mozzarella, sliced thinly
3 anchovies, halved lengthways
2 tsp capers
4 pitted black olives, sliced
4 fresh basil leaves, shredded
olive oil for drizzling
salt and pepper

1 Roll out or press the dough, using a rolling pin or your hands, into a 25 cm/10 inch circle on a lightly floured surface. Place on a large greased baking sheet (cookie sheet) or pizza pan and push up the edge a little.

2 Cover and leave to rise slightly for 10 minutes in a warm place before spreading with tomato sauce almost to the edge.

3 Put the sliced chorizo on to one quarter of the pizza, the sliced mushrooms on another, the artichoke hearts on a third, and the Mozzarella and anchovies on the fourth.

4 Dot the with the capers, olives and basil leaves. Drizzle with a little olive oil and season. Do not put any salt on the anchovy section as the fish are very salty.

5 Bake in a preheated oven, 200°C/400°F/Gas Mark 6, for 18–20 minutes, or until the crust is golden and crisp. Serve immediately.

Step *1*

Step *3*

Step *4*

Calabrian Pizza

Traditionally, this pizza has a double layer of dough to make it robust and filling. Alternatively, it can be made as a single pizza (as shown here).

SERVES 4-6

INGREDIENTS

425 g/14 oz/3½ cups plain (all-purpose) flour
½ tsp salt
1 sachet easy-blend yeast
2 tbsp olive oil
about 275 ml/9 fl oz/generous 1 cup warm water

FILLING

2 tbsp olive oil
2 garlic cloves, crushed
1 red (bell) pepper, cored, deseeded and sliced
1 yellow (bell) pepper, cored, deseeded
and sliced
125 g/4 oz Ricotta
175 g/6 oz jar sun-dried tomatoes,
drained
3 hard-boiled (hard-cooked) eggs, sliced thinly
1 tbsp chopped fresh mixed herbs
125 g/4 oz salami, cut into strips
150–175 g/5–6 oz Mozzarella, grated
a little milk, to glaze
salt and pepper

1 Sift the flour and salt into a bowl and mix in the easy-blend yeast. Add the olive oil and enough warm water to mix to a smooth pliable dough. Knead for 10–15 minutes by hand, or process for 5 minutes in a mixer.

2 Shape the dough into a ball, place in a lightly oiled polythene bag and put in a warm place for 1–1½ hours or until doubled in size.

3 For the filling: heat the oil in a frying pan (skillet) and fry the garlic and (bell) peppers slowly in the oil until soft.

4 Knock back the dough and roll out half to fit the base of a 30 × 25 cm/12 × 10 inch oiled roasting tin.

5 Season the dough and spread with the Ricotta, then cover with sun-dried tomatoes, hard-boiled eggs, herbs and the pepper mixture. Arrange the salami strips on top and sprinkle with the grated cheese.

6 Roll out the remaining dough and place over the filling, sealing the edges well, or use to make a second pizza. Leave to rise for 1 hour in a warm place. An uncovered pizza will only take about 30–40 minutes to rise.

7 Prick the double pizza with a fork about 20 times, brush the top with milk and cook in a preheated oven, 180°C/350°F/Gas Mark 4, for about 50 minutes or until lightly browned. The uncovered pizza will take only 35–40 minutes. Serve hot.

Step *1*

Step *4*

Step *5*

Smoky Bacon & Peperoni

This more traditional kind of pizza is topped with peperoni, smoked bacon and (bell) peppers covered in a smoked cheese.

SERVES 2–4

INGREDIENTS

Bread Dough Base (page 186)
1 tbsp olive oil
1 tbsp freshly grated Parmesan
Tomato Sauce (page 192)
125 g/4 oz lightly smoked bacon, diced
½ green (bell) pepper, sliced thinly
½ yellow (bell) pepper, sliced thinly
60 g/2 oz peperoni-style sliced spicy sausage
60 g/2 oz smoked Bavarian cheese, grated
½ tsp dried oregano
olive oil for drizzling
salt and pepper

1 Roll out or press the dough, using a rolling pin or your hands, into a 25 cm/10 inch circle on a lightly floured work surface. Place on a large greased baking sheet (cookie sheet) or pizza pan and push up the edge a little with your fingers, to form a rim.

2 Brush the base with the olive oil and sprinkle with the Parmesan. Cover and leave to rise slightly in a warm place for about 10 minutes.

3 Spread the tomato sauce over the base almost to the edge. Top with the bacon and (bell) peppers. Arrange the peperoni on top and sprinkle with the smoked cheese.

4 Sprinkle over the oregano and drizzle with a little olive oil. Season well.

5 Bake in a preheated oven, 200°C/400°F/Gas Mark 6, for 18–20 minutes, or until the crust is golden and crisp around the edge. Cut into wedges and serve immediately.

Step *2*

Step *3*

Step *4*

Calzone

A calzone is like a pizza in reverse – it resembles a large pasty with the dough on the outside and the filling on the inside.

SERVES 2–4

INGREDIENTS

Bread Dough Base (page 186)
1 egg, beaten
1 tomato, peeled and chopped
1 tbsp tomato purée
30 g/1 oz Italian salami, chopped
30 g/1 oz mortadella ham, chopped
30 g/1 oz Ricotta
2 spring onions (scallions),
trimmed and chopped
¼ tsp dried oregano
salt and pepper

1 Roll out the dough into a 23 cm/9 inch circle on a lightly floured work surface. Brush the edge of the dough with a little beaten egg.

2 Spread the tomato purée over half the circle nearest to you. Scatter the salami, mortadella and chopped tomato on top. Dot with the Ricotta and sprinkle over the spring onions (scallions) and oregano. Season well.

3 Fold over the other half of the dough to form a half moon. Press the edges together well to prevent the filling from coming out.

4 Place on a baking sheet (cookie sheet) and brush with beaten egg to glaze. Make a hole in the top to allow steam to escape.

5 Bake in a preheated oven, 200°C/400°F/Gas Mark 6, for 20 minutes, or until golden.

Step *1*

Step *2*

Step *3*

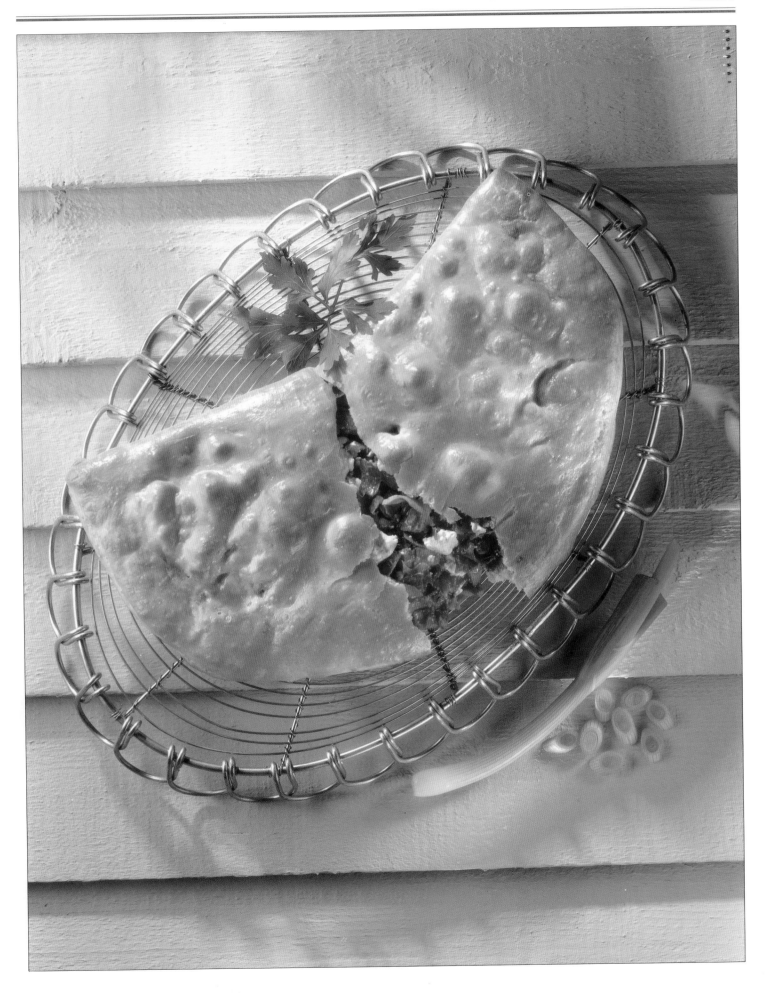

Avocado & Ham

*A smoked ham and avocado salad is served on a pizza with a base
enriched with chopped sun-dried tomatoes and black olives.*

SERVES 2-4

INGREDIENTS

Bread Dough Base (page 186)
4 sun-dried tomatoes, chopped
30 g/1 oz black olives, chopped
Special Tomato Sauce (page 194)
4 small chicory (endive) leaves, shredded
4 small radicchio leaves, shredded
1 avocado, peeled, pitted and sliced
60 g/2 oz wafer-thin smoked ham
60 g/2 oz blue cheese,
cut into small pieces
olive oil for drizzling
salt and pepper
chopped fresh chervil, to garnish

1 Knead the dough gently with the sun-dried tomatoes and olives until well mixed.

2 Roll out or press the dough, using a rolling pin or your hands, into a 25 cm/10 inch circle on a lightly floured work surface. Place on a greased baking sheet (cookie sheet) or pizza pan and push up the edge a little to form a rim.

3 Cover and leave to rise slightly in a warm place for 10 minutes before spreading with tomato sauce almost to the edge.

4 Top the pizza with shredded lettuce leaves and avocado slices. Scrunch up the ham and add with the cheese. Drizzle with a little olive oil and season well.

5 Bake in a preheated oven, 200°C/400°F/Gas Mark 6, for 18–20 minutes, or until the edge is crisp and golden brown.

6 Sprinkle with chervil to garnish and serve immediately.

Step *1*

Step *3*

Step *6*

Spicy Meatball

*Small minced (ground) beef meatballs, spiced with chillies and
cumin seeds, are baked on a scone (biscuit) base.*

SERVES 2-4

INGREDIENTS

250 g/8 oz minced (ground) lean beef
30 g/1 oz jalapeño chillies in brine, chopped
1 tsp cumin seeds
1 tbsp chopped fresh parsley
1 tbsp beaten egg
3 tbsp olive oil
Scone (Biscuit) Base (page 188)
Tomato Sauce (page 192)
30 g/1 oz canned pimiento, sliced
2 rashers streaky bacon, cut into strips
60 g/2 oz mature (sharp) Cheddar, grated
olive oil for drizzling
salt and pepper
chopped fresh parsley, to garnish

1 Mix the beef, chillies, cumin seeds, parsley and egg together in a bowl and season. Form into 12 small meatballs. Cover and chill for 1 hour.

2 Heat the oil in a large frying pan (skillet). Add the meatballs and brown all over. Remove with a perforated spoon or fish slice and drain on paper towels.

3 Roll out or press the dough into a 25 cm/10 inch circle on a lightly floured work surface. Place on a greased baking sheet (cookie sheet) or pizza pan and push up the edge slightly to form a rim. Spread with the tomato sauce almost to the edge.

4 Arrange the meatballs on the pizza with the pimiento and bacon. Sprinkle over the cheese and drizzle with a little olive oil. Season.

5 Bake in a preheated oven, 200°C/400°F/Gas Mark 6, for 18–20 minutes, or until the edge is golden and crisp. Serve immediately, garnished with chopped parsley.

Step *2*

Step *3*

Step *4*

American Hot Chilli Beef

This deep-pan pizza is topped with minced (ground) beef, red kidney beans and jalapeño chillies, which are small, green and very hot.

SERVES 2-4

INGREDIENTS

FOR THE DOUGH BASE

20 g/¾ oz fresh yeast or 1½ tsp dried or easy-blend yeast
125 ml/4 fl oz/½ cup tepid water
1 tsp sugar
3 tbsp olive oil
250 g/8 oz/2 cups plain (all-purpose) flour
1 tsp salt

FOR THE TOPPING

1 small onion, sliced thinly
1 garlic clove, crushed
½ yellow (bell) pepper, chopped
1 tbsp olive oil
175 g/6 oz lean minced (ground) beef
¼ tsp chilli powder
¼ tsp ground cumin
200 g/7 oz can red kidney beans, drained
Tomato Sauce (page 192)
30 g/1 oz jalapeño chillies, sliced
60 g/2 oz Mozzarella, sliced thinly
60 g/2 oz mature (sharp) Cheddar or Monterey Jack, grated
olive oil for drizzling
salt and pepper
chopped parsley, to garnish

1 For the deep-pan dough base, use the same method as the Bread Dough Base recipe (page 186).

2 Roll out or press the dough, using a rolling pin or your hands, into a 23 cm/9 inch circle on a lightly floured work surface. Place on a large greased baking sheet (cookie sheet) or pizza pan and push up the edge to form a small ridge. Cover and leave to rise slightly for about 10 minutes.

3 Fry the onion, garlic and (bell) pepper gently in the oil for 5 minutes until soft but not browned. Increase the heat slightly and add the beef, chilli and cumin. Fry for 5 minutes, stirring occasionally. Remove from the heat and stir in the kidney beans. Season well.

4 Spread the tomato sauce over the dough almost to the edge and top with the meat mixture.

5 Top with the sliced chillies and Mozzarella and sprinkle over the grated cheese. Drizzle with a little olive oil and season.

6 Bake in a preheated oven, 200°C/400°F/Gas Mark 6, for 18–20 minutes, or until the crust is golden. Serve immediately sprinkled with chopped parsley.

Step *3*

Step *4*

Step *5*

Breakfast Pizza

*Sausages, bacon and mushrooms on a bread base topped with a fried egg
will probably see you through the day.*

SERVES 4

INGREDIENTS

Bread Dough Base (page 186)
12 skinless cocktail sausages
3 tbsp oil
Tomato Sauce (page 192)
150 g/5 oz can baked beans
4 rashers back bacon
60 g/2 oz baby button mushrooms, wiped
and quartered
1 small tomato, cut into 8 wedges
60 g/2 oz mature (sharp) Cheddar, grated
4 eggs
salt and pepper

1 Roll out or press the dough, using a rolling pin or your hands, into a 25 cm/10 inch circle on a lightly floured work surface. Place on a large greased baking sheet (cookie sheet) or pizza pan and push up the edge slightly to form a rim. Cover and leave to rise slightly for 10 minutes in a warm place.

2 Brown the sausages in a frying pan (skillet) with 1 tablespoon of the oil.

3 Mix the tomato sauce with the baked beans and spread over the base almost to the edge. Arrange the sausages on top.

4 Cut the bacon into strips and arrange on the pizza with the mushrooms and tomato. Sprinkle over the cheese and season.

5 Bake in a preheated oven, 200°C/400°F/Gas Mark 6, for 18–20 minutes, or until the edge is crisp and golden brown.

6 Add the remaining oil to the pan and fry the eggs. When the pizza is cooked, cut into four and top each with a fried egg. Serve immediately.

Step *3*

Step *4*

Step *6*

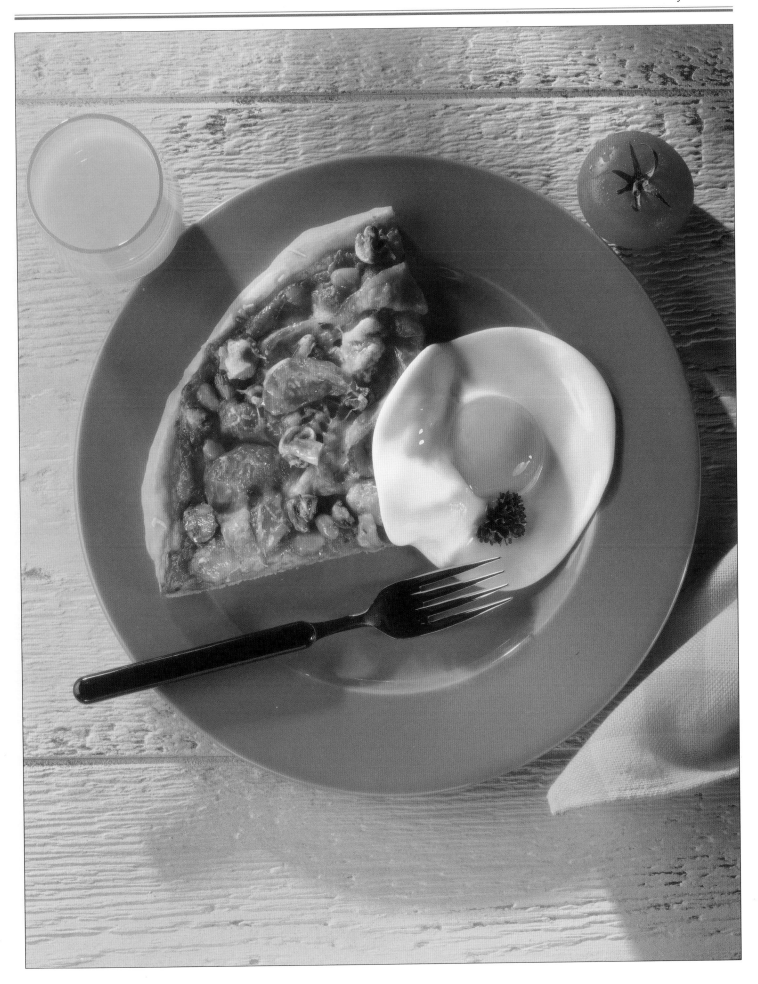

Funny Faces

These individual pizzas have faces made from sliced vegetables and pasta.
Children love pizzas and will enjoy making their own funny faces.

SERVES 4

INGREDIENTS

Bread Dough Base (page 186)
30 g/1 oz spaghetti or egg noodles
Tomato Sauce (page 192)
8 slices peperoni-style sausage
8 thin slices celery
4 slices button mushrooms
4 slices yellow (bell) pepper
4 slices Mozzarella
4 slices courgette (zucchini)
olive oil for drizzling
8 peas

1 Divide the dough into four. Roll each piece out into a 12 cm/5 inch diameter circle and place on greased baking sheets (cookie sheets). Cover and leave to rise slightly in a warm place for about 10 minutes.

2 Cook the spaghetti or egg noodles according to the packet instructions.

3 Divide the tomato sauce evenly between each pizza base and spread out almost to the edge.

4 To make the faces, use peperoni slices for the main part of the eyes, celery for the eyebrows, mushrooms for the noses and (bell) pepper slices for the mouths.

5 Cut the Mozzarella and courgette (zucchini) slices in half. Use the cheese for the cheeks and the courgettes (zucchini) for the ears.

6 Drizzle a little olive oil over each pizza and bake in a preheated oven, 200°C/400°F/Gas Mark 6, for 12–15 minutes until the edges are crisp and golden.

7 Transfer the pizzas to serving plates and place the peas in the centre of the eyes. Drain the spaghetti or noodles and arrange around the tops of the pizzas for hair. Serve immediately.

Step *4*

Step *6*

Step *7*

Aubergine (Eggplant) & Lamb

An unusual fragrant, spiced pizza topped with minced (ground) lamb and aubergine (eggplant) on a bread base.

SERVES 2–4

INGREDIENTS

1 small aubergine (eggplant), diced
Bread Dough Base (page 186)
1 small onion, sliced thinly
1 garlic clove, crushed
1 tsp cumin seeds
1 tbsp olive oil
175 g/6 oz minced (ground) lamb
30 g/1 oz canned pimiento, thinly sliced
2 tbsp chopped fresh coriander (cilantro)
Special Tomato Sauce (page 194)
90 g/3 oz Mozzarella, sliced thinly
olive oil for drizzling
salt and pepper

1 Sprinkle the diced aubergine (eggplant) with salt in a colander and let the bitter juices drain for about 20 minutes; then rinse. Pat dry with paper towels.

2 Roll out or press the dough, using a rolling pin or your hands, into a 25 cm/10 inch circle on a lightly floured work surface. Place on a large greased baking sheet (cookie sheet) or pizza pan and push up the edge to form a rim.

3 Cover and leave to rise slightly for 10 minutes in a warm place.

4 Fry the onion, garlic and cumin seeds gently in the oil for 3 minutes. Increase the heat slightly and add the lamb, aubergine (eggplant) and pimiento. Fry for 5 minutes, stirring occasionally. Add the coriander (cilantro) and season well.

5 Spread the tomato sauce over the dough base almost to the edge. Top with the lamb mixture.

6 Arrange the Mozzarella slices on top. Drizzle over a little olive oil and season.

7 Bake in a preheated oven, 200°C/400°F/Gas Mark 6, for 18–20 minutes, until the crust is crisp and golden. Serve immediately.

Step *1*

Step *4*

Step *6*

Marinara

This pizza is topped with frozen mixed seafood such as prawns (shrimp), mussels, cockles and squid rings.

SERVES 2–4

INGREDIENTS

Potato Base (page 190)
Special Tomato Sauce (page 194)
200 g/7 oz frozen seafood cocktail, defrosted
1 tbsp capers
1 small yellow (bell) pepper, chopped
1 tbsp chopped fresh marjoram
½ tsp dried oregano
60 g/2 oz Mozzarella, grated
15 g/½ oz Parmesan, grated
12 black olives
olive oil for drizzling
salt and pepper
sprig of fresh marjoram or oregano, to garnish

1 Roll out or press out the potato dough, using a rolling pin or your hands, into a 25 cm/10 inch circle on a lightly floured work surface. Place on a large greased baking sheet (cookie sheet) or pizza pan and push up the edge a little with your fingers to form a rim.

2 Spread the tomato sauce evenly over the base almost to the edge.

3 Arrange the seafood cocktail, capers and yellow (bell) pepper on top of the sauce.

4 Sprinkle over the herbs and cheeses. Arrange the olives on top. Drizzle over a little olive oil and season generously with salt and pepper.

5 Bake in a preheated oven, 200°C/400°F/Gas Mark 6, for 18–20 minutes until the edge of the pizza is crisp and golden brown.

6 Transfer to a warmed serving plate, garnish with a sprig of marjoram or oregano and serve immediately.

Step *2*

Step *3*

Step *4*

Florentine

*A pizza adaptation of Eggs Florentine – sliced hard-boiled (hard-cooked)
eggs on freshly cooked spinach, with a crunchy almond topping.*

SERVES 2–4

INGREDIENTS

2 tbsp freshly grated Parmesan
Potato Base (page 190)
Tomato Sauce (page 192)
175 g/6 oz spinach
1 small red onion, sliced thinly
2 tbsp olive oil
¼ tsp freshly grated nutmeg
2 hard-boiled (hard-cooked) eggs
15 g/½ oz fresh white breadcrumbs
60 g/2 oz Jarlsberg, grated (or Cheddar or
Gruyère, if not available)
2 tbsp flaked (slivered) almonds
olive oil for drizzling
salt and pepper

1 Mix the Parmesan with the potato base. Roll out or press the dough, using a rolling pin or your hands, into a 25 cm/10 inch circle on a lightly floured work surface. Place on a large greased baking sheet (cookie sheet) or pizza pan and push up the edge slightly. Spread the tomato sauce almost to the edge.

2 Remove the stalks from the spinach and wash the leaves thoroughly in plenty of cold water. Drain well and pat off the excess water with paper towels.

3 Fry the onion gently in the oil for 5 minutes until softened. Add the spinach and continue to fry until just wilted. Drain off any excess liquid. Place on the pizza and sprinkle over the nutmeg.

4 Remove the shells from the eggs and slice. Arrange on top of the spinach.

5 Mix together the breadcrumbs, cheese and almonds, and sprinkle over. Drizzle with a little olive oil and season well.

6 Bake in a preheated oven, 200°C/400°F/Gas Mark 6, for 18–20 minutes, or until the edge is crisp and golden. Serve immediately.

Step *1*

Step *3*

Step *4*

Alaska Pizza

You can use either red or pink canned salmon to top this tasty pizza.
Red salmon has a better colour and flavour but it can be expensive.

SERVES 2–4

INGREDIENTS

Scone (Biscuit) Base (page 188)
Tomato Sauce (page 192)
1 courgette (zucchini), grated
1 tomato, sliced thinly
100 g/3½ oz can red or pink salmon, drained
60 g/2 oz button mushrooms, wiped and sliced
1 tbsp chopped fresh dill
½ tsp dried oregano
45 g/1½ oz Mozzarella, grated
olive oil for drizzling
salt and pepper
sprig of fresh dill, to garnish

1 Roll out or press the dough, using a rolling pin or your hands, into a 25 cm/10 inch circle on a lightly floured work surface. Place on a large greased baking sheet, or pizza pan and push up the edge a little with your fingers to form a rim.

2 Spread the tomato sauce evenly over the pizza almost to the edge.

3 Sprinkle the tomato sauce with the grated courgette (zucchini), then lay the tomato slices on top.

4 Remove any bones and skin from the salmon and flake. Arrange on the pizza with the mushrooms. Sprinkle over the herbs and cheese. Drizzle with a little olive oil and season well.

5 Bake in a preheated oven, 200°C/400°F/Gas Mark 6, for 18–20 minutes, or until the edge is golden and crisp. Transfer to a warmed serving plate and serve immediately, garnished with a sprig of dill.

Step *3*

Step *4*

Step *5*

Herbed Onion with Anchovies

This tasty onion pizza is topped with a lattice pattern of anchovies and black olives. Cut the pizza into squares to serve.

MAKES 6 SQUARES

INGREDIENTS

4 tbsp olive oil
3 onions, sliced thinly
1 garlic clove, crushed
1tsp soft brown sugar
½ tsp crushed fresh rosemary
200 g/7 oz can chopped tomatoes
Bread Dough Base (page 186)
2 tbsp freshly grated Parmesan
50 g/1¾ oz can anchovies
12–14 black olives
salt and pepper

1 Heat 3 tablespoons of the oil in a large saucepan and add the onions, garlic, sugar and rosemary. Cover and fry gently for 10 minutes until the onions are soft but not brown, stirring occasionally. Add the tomatoes, stir and season well. Leave to cool slightly.

2 Roll out or press the dough, using a rolling pin or your hands, on a lightly floured work surface to fit a 30 × 18 cm/12 × 7 inch greased Swiss roll tin. Place in the tin and push up the edges slightly.

3 Brush the remaining oil over the dough and sprinkle with the cheese. Cover and leave to rise slightly in a warm place for about 10 minutes.

4 Spread the onion and tomato topping over the base. Drain the anchovies, reserving the oil. Split each anchovy in half lengthways and arrange on the pizza in a lattice pattern. Place olives in between the anchovies and drizzle over a little of the reserved oil. Season.

5 Bake in a preheated oven, 200°C/400°F/Gas Mark 6, for 18–20 minutes, or until the edges are crisp and golden. Cut into squares and serve immediately.

Step *1*

Step *2*

Step *4*

Roasted Vegetable & Goat's Cheese

Wonderfully colourful vegetables are roasted in olive oil with thyme and garlic. The goat's cheese adds a nutty, piquant flavour.

SERVES 2–4

INGREDIENTS

2 baby courgettes (zucchini),
halved lengthways
2 baby aubergines (eggplant),
quartered lengthways
½ red (bell) pepper, cut into 4 strips
½ yellow (bell) pepper, cut into 4 strips
1 small red onion, cut into wedges
2 garlic cloves, unpeeled
4 tbsp olive oil
1 tbsp red wine vinegar
1 tbsp chopped fresh thyme
Bread Dough Base (page 186)
Tomato Sauce (page 192)
90 g/3 oz goat's cheese
salt and pepper
fresh basil leaves, to garnish

1 Place all the prepared vegetables in a large roasting tin. Mix together the olive oil, vinegar, thyme and plenty of seasoning and pour over, coating well.

2 Roast the vegetables in a preheated oven, 200°C/400°F/Gas Mark 6, for 15–20 minutes until the skins have started to blacken in places, turning half-way through. Leave to rest for 5 minutes after roasting.

3 Carefully peel off the skins from the roast (bell) peppers and the garlic cloves. Slice the garlic.

4 Roll out or press the dough, using a rolling pin or your hands, into a 25 cm/10 inch circle on a lightly floured work surface. Place on a large greased baking sheet (cookie sheet) or pizza pan and raise the edge a little. Cover and leave for 10 minutes to rise slightly in a warm place. Spread with the tomato sauce almost to the edge.

5 Arrange the roasted vegetables on top and dot with the cheese. Drizzle the oil and juices from the roasting tin over the pizza and season.

6 Bake in a preheated oven, 200°C/400°F/Gas Mark 6, for 18–20 minutes, or until the edge is crisp and golden. Serve immediately garnished with basil leaves.

Step *1*

Step *3*

Step *5*

Mixed (Bell) Peppers & Red Onion

The vibrant colours of the (bell) peppers and onion make this a delightful pizza. Served cut into fingers, it is ideal for a party or buffet.

MAKES 8

INGREDIENTS

Bread Dough Base (page 186)
2 tbsp olive oil
½ each red, green and yellow (bell) pepper,
sliced thinly
1 small red onion, sliced thinly
1 garlic clove, crushed
Tomato Sauce (page 192)
3 tbsp raisins
30 g/1 oz pine kernels (nuts)
1 tbsp chopped fresh thyme
olive oil for drizzling
salt and pepper

1 Roll out or press the dough, using a rolling pin or your hands, on a lightly floured work surface to fit a 30 × 18 cm/12 × 7 inch greased Swiss roll tin. Place in the tin and push up the edges slightly.

2 Cover and leave to rise slightly in a warm place for about 10 minutes.

3 Heat the oil in a large frying pan (skillet). Add the (bell) peppers, onion and garlic, and fry gently for 5 minutes until they have softened but not browned. Leave to cool.

4 Spread the tomato sauce over the base of the pizza almost to the edge.

5 Sprinkle over the raisins and top with the cooled (bell) pepper mixture. Add the pine kernels (nuts) and thyme. Drizzle with a little olive oil and season well.

6 Bake in a preheated oven, 200°C/400°F/Gas Mark 6, for 18–20 minutes, or until the edges are crisp and golden. Cut into fingers and serve immediately.

Step *3*

Step *5*

Step *6*

French Bread Pizzas

Halved baguettes or ciabatta bread are a ready-made pizza base. The colours of the tomatoes and cheese contrast beautifully on top.

SERVES 4

INGREDIENTS

2 sticks of French bread
Tomato Sauce (page 192)
4 plum tomatoes, sliced thinly lengthways
150 g/5 oz Mozzarella, sliced thinly
10 black olives, cut into rings
8 fresh basil leaves, shredded
olive oil for drizzling
salt and pepper

1 Cut the baguettes in half lengthways and toast the cut side of the bread lightly. Spread the toasted baguettes with the tomato sauce.

2 Arrange the tomato and Mozzarella slices alternately along the length.

3 Top with the olive rings and half the basil. Drizzle over a little olive oil and season well.

4 Either place under a preheated medium grill (broiler) and cook until the cheese is melted and bubbling or bake in a preheated oven, 200°C/400°F/Gas Mark 6, for 15–20 minutes.

5 Sprinkle over the remaining basil and serve immediately.

Step *1*

Step *2*

Step *3*

Giardiniera

As the name implies, this colourful pizza should be topped with fresh vegetables from the garden, especially in the summer months.

SERVES 2-4

INGREDIENTS

6 spinach leaves
Potato Base (page 190)
Special Tomato Sauce (page 194)
1 tomato, sliced
1 celery stalk, sliced thinly
½ green (bell) pepper, sliced thinly
1 baby courgette (zucchini), sliced
30 g/1 oz asparagus tips
30 g/1 oz sweetcorn, defrosted if frozen
30 g/1 oz peas, defrosted if frozen
4 spring onions (scallions), trimmed
and chopped
1 tbsp chopped fresh mixed herbs
60 g/2 oz Mozzarella, grated
2 tbsp freshly grated Parmesan
1 artichoke heart
olive oil for drizzling
salt and pepper

1 Remove any tough stalks from the spinach and wash the leaves in plenty of cold water. Pat dry with paper towels.

2 Roll out or press the potato base, using a rolling pin or your hands, into a large 25 cm/10 inch circle on a lightly floured work surface. Place the round on a large greased baking sheet (cookie sheet) or pizza pan and push up the edge a little. Spread with the tomato sauce.

3 Arrange the spinach leaves on the sauce, followed by the tomato slices. Top with the remaining vegetables and the herbs.

4 Mix together the cheeses and sprinkle over. Place the artichoke heart in the centre. Drizzle the pizza with a little olive oil and season.

5 Bake in a preheated oven, 200°C/400°F/Gas Mark 6, for 18–20 minutes, or until the edges are crisp and golden brown. Serve immediately.

Step *1*

Step *3*

Step *4*

Wild Mushroom & Walnut

*Wild mushrooms make a delicious pizza topping when mixed
with walnuts and Roquefort cheese.*

SERVES 2–4

INGREDIENTS

Scone (Biscuit) Base (page 188)
Special Tomato Sauce (page 194)
125 g/4 oz soft cheese
1 tbsp chopped fresh mixed herbs, such as
parsley, oregano and basil
250 g/8 oz wild mushrooms, such as oyster,
shiitake or ceps, or 125 g/4 oz each wild
and button mushrooms
2 tbsp olive oil
¼ tsp fennel seeds
30 g/1 oz walnuts, chopped roughly
45 g/1½ oz blue cheese
olive oil for drizzling
salt and pepper
sprig of flat-leaf parsley, to garnish

1 Roll out or press the scone (biscuit) base, using a rolling pin or your hands, into a 25 cm/10 inch circle on a lightly floured work surface. Place on a large greased baking sheet (cookie sheet) or pizza pan and push up the edge a little with your fingers to form a rim.

2 Spread with the tomato sauce almost to the edge. Dot with the soft cheese and herbs.

3 Wipe and slice the mushrooms. Heat the oil in a large frying pan (skillet) or wok and stir-fry the mushrooms and fennel seeds for 2–3 minutes. Spread over the pizza with the walnuts.

4 Crumble the cheese over the pizza, drizzle with a little olive oil and season.

5 Bake in a preheated oven, 200°C/400°F/Gas Mark 6, for 18–20 minutes, or until the edge is crisp and golden. Serve immediately, garnished with a sprig of flat-leaf parsley.

Step *2*

Step *3*

Step *4*

Ratatouille & Lentil

The ideal vegetarian pizza. Ratatouille and lentils on a wholemeal bread base are topped with vegetarian cheese and sunflower seeds.

SERVES 2-4

INGREDIENTS

60 g/2 oz green lentils
½ small aubergine (eggplant), diced
1 small onion, sliced
1 garlic clove, crushed
3 tbsp olive oil
½ courgette (zucchini), sliced
½ red (bell) pepper, sliced
½ green (bell) pepper, sliced
200 g/7 oz can chopped tomatoes
1 tbsp chopped fresh oregano or 1 tsp dried
Bread Dough Base made with
wholemeal flour (page 186)
60 g/2 oz vegetarian Cheddar, sliced thinly
1 tbsp sunflower seeds
olive oil for drizzling
salt and pepper

1 Soak the lentils in hot water for 30 minutes. Drain and rinse; then cover with fresh water and simmer for 10 minutes.

2 Sprinkle the aubergine (eggplant) with a little salt in a colander and leave the bitter juices to drain for about 20 minutes. Rinse and pat dry with paper towels.

3 Fry the onion and garlic gently in the oil for 3 minutes. Add the courgette (zucchini), (bell) peppers and aubergine (eggplant). Cover and leave to cook over a low heat for about 5 minutes.

4 Add the tomatoes, drained lentils, oregano, 2 tablespoons of water and seasoning. Cover and simmer for 15 minutes, stirring occasionally, adding more water if necessary.

5 Roll out or press the dough, using a rolling pin or your hands, into a 25 cm/10 inch circle on a lightly floured work surface. Place on a large greased baking sheet (cookie sheet) or pizza pan and push up the edge slightly. Cover and leave to rise slightly for 10 minutes in a warm place.

6 Spread the ratatouille over the dough base almost to the edge. Arrange the cheese slices on top and sprinkle over the sunflower seeds. Drizzle with a little olive oil and season.

7 Bake in a preheated oven, 200°C/400°F/Gas Mark 6, for 18–20 minutes, or until the edge is crisp and golden brown. Serve immediately.

Step *1*

Step *3*

Step *6*

Tofu with Sweetcorn & Peas

*Chunks of tofu marinated in ginger and soy sauce impart something
of an oriental flavour to this pizza.*

SERVES 2-4

INGREDIENTS

1 litre/1¾ pints milk
1 tsp salt
250 g/8 oz semolina
1 tbsp soy sauce
1 tbsp dry sherry
½ tsp grated fresh ginger root
275 g/9 oz tofu, cut into chunks
2 eggs
60 g/2 oz Parmesan, grated
Tomato Sauce (page 192)
30 g/1 oz baby sweetcorn, cut into 4
30 g/1 oz mangetout (snow peas),
trimmed and cut into 4
4 spring onions (scallions), trimmed and
cut into 2.5 cm/1 inch strips
60 g/2 oz Mozzarella, sliced thinly
2 tsp sesame oil
salt and pepper

1 Bring the milk to the boil with the salt. Sprinkle the semolina over the surface, stirring all the time. Cook for 10 minutes over a low heat, stirring occasionally, taking care not to let it burn. Remove from the heat and leave to cool until tepid.

2 Mix the soy sauce, sherry and ginger together in a bowl, add the tofu and stir gently to coat. Leave to marinate in a cool place for about 20 minutes.

3 Beat the eggs with a little pepper. Add to the semolina with the Parmesan and mix well. Place on a large greased baking sheet (cookie sheet) or pizza pan and pat into a 25 cm/10 inch round, using the back of a metal spoon. Spread the tomato sauce almost to the edge.

4 Blanch the sweetcorn and mangetout (snow peas) in boiling water for 1 minute, drain and place on the pizza with the drained tofu. Top with the spring onions (scallions) and slices of cheese. Drizzle over the sesame oil and season.

5 Bake in a preheated oven, 200°C/400°F/Gas Mark 6, for 18–20 minutes, or until the edge is crisp and golden. Serve immediately.

Step *1*

Step *2*

Step *4*

Three Cheese & Artichoke

Sliced artichokes combined with mature (sharp) Cheddar, Parmesan and blue cheese give a really delicious topping to this pizza.

SERVES 2-4

INGREDIENTS

Bread Dough Base (page 186)
Special Tomato Sauce (page 194)
60 g/2 oz blue cheese, sliced
125 g/4 oz artichoke hearts in oil, sliced
½ small red onion, chopped
45 g/1½ oz mature (sharp) cheese, grated
2 tbsp freshly grated Parmesan
1 tbsp chopped fresh thyme
oil from artichokes for drizzling
salt and pepper

TO SERVE

salad leaves
cherry tomatoes, halved

1 Roll out or press the dough, using a rolling pin or your hands, into a 25 cm/10 inch circle on a lightly floured work surface. Place the base on a large greased baking sheet (cookie sheet) or pizza pan and push up the edge slightly. Cover and leave to rise for 10 minutes in a warm place.

2 Spread with the tomato sauce almost to the edge. Arrange the blue cheese on the tomato sauce, followed by the artichoke hearts and red onion.

3 Mix the Cheddar and Parmesan cheeses together with the thyme and sprinkle the mixture over the pizza. Drizzle a little of the oil from the jar of artichokes over the pizza and season to taste.

4 Bake in a preheated oven, 200°C/400°F/Gas Mark 6, for 18–20 minutes, or until the edge is crisp and golden and the cheese is bubbling.

5 Serve immediately with fresh salad leaves and cherry tomato halves.

Step *2*

Step *3*

Step *5*

DESSERTS

Many Italians prefer to finish their meal with a bowl of mixed fruits or fruits with cheese, but they do like their desserts too. When there is a family gathering or celebration, then a special effort is made and the delicacies appear. The Sicilians are said to have the sweetest tooth of all, and many Italian desserts are thought to have originated there. You have to go a very long way to beat a Sicilian ice-cream, especially the famous cassata and Ricotta ice-creams.

Fruits also feature in desserts. The mouthwatering pear tarts from northern Italy use the very best fruit blended with apricot jam, sultanas and almonds. Oranges are often peeled and served whole, marinated in a fragrant syrup and liqueur. Almond-flavoured biscuits are often served as an accompaniment, and the famous Florentines – biscuits packed with glacé fruit and covered with chocolate – are a special favourite. Gâteaux are popular, often incorporating mascarpone or Ricotta cheese together with citrus fruits and honey. Tiramisu is an all-time favourite, and for Christmas and special occasions try the honey cake from Siena called Panforte – so very rich that even a tiny piece will leave you with delicious memories for a very long time.

Tiramisu

A favourite Italian dessert flavoured with coffee and Amaretto. You could
substitute the Amaretto with brandy or Marsala.

SERVES 4–6

INGREDIENTS

20–24 sponge fingers (lady-fingers),
about 150 g/5 oz
2 tbsp cold black coffee
2 tbsp coffee essence
2 tbsp Amaretto
4 egg yolks
90 g/3 oz/6 tbsp caster (superfine) sugar
few drops of vanilla essence
grated rind of ½ lemon
350 g/12 oz/1½ cups Mascarpone cheese
(Italian full-fat cream cheese)
2 tsp lemon juice
250 ml/8 fl oz/1 cup double (heavy) cream
1 tbsp milk
30 g/1 oz/½ cup flaked (slivered) almonds,
lightly toasted
2 tbsp cocoa powder
1 tbsp icing (confectioners') sugar

1 Arrange almost half the sponge fingers (lady-fingers) in the base of a glass bowl or serving dish.

2 Combine the black coffee, coffee essence and Amaretto and sprinkle just over half the mixture over the fingers.

3 Put the egg yolks into a heatproof bowl with the sugar, vanilla essence and lemon rind. Stand over a saucepan of gently simmering water and whisk until very thick and creamy and the whisk leaves a very heavy trail when lifted from the bowl.

4 Put the Mascarpone cheese in a bowl with the lemon juice and beat until smooth.

5 Combine the egg and Mascarpone cheese mixtures and when evenly blended pour half over the sponge fingers (lady-fingers) and spread out evenly.

6 Add another layer of fingers, sprinkle with the remaining coffee and then cover with the rest of the cheese mixture. Chill for at least 2 hours and preferably longer, or overnight.

7 To serve, whip the cream and milk together until fairly stiff and spread or pipe over the dessert. Sprinkle with the flaked (slivered) almonds and then sift an even layer of cocoa powder so the top is completely covered. Finally sift a light layer of icing sugar over the cocoa.

Step *2*

Step *3*

Step *6*

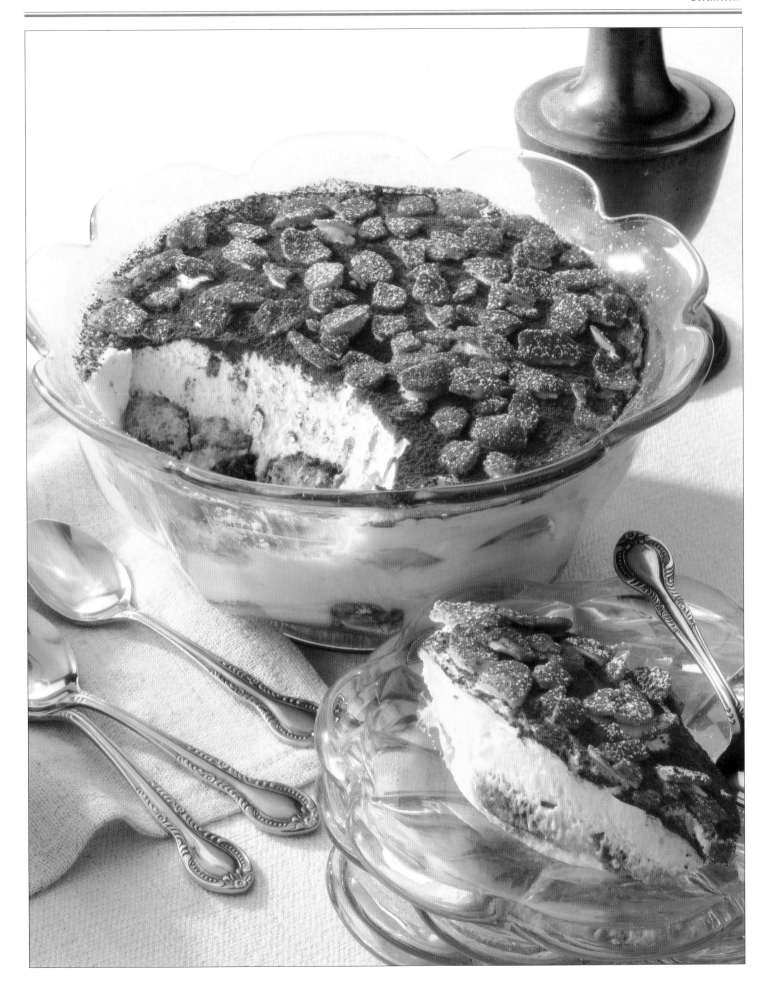

Zabaglione

*Serve this light dessert warm or chilled, accompanied by sponge fingers
(lady-fingers) or amaretti biscuits, and soft fruits.*

SERVES 4

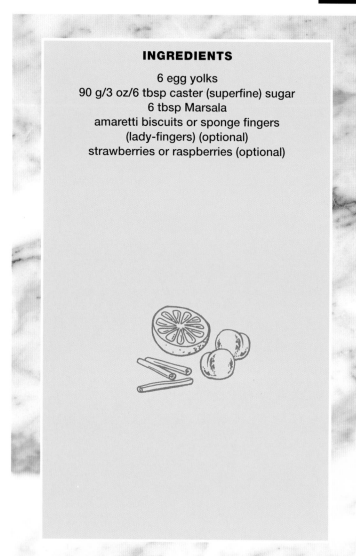

INGREDIENTS

6 egg yolks
90 g/3 oz/6 tbsp caster (superfine) sugar
6 tbsp Marsala
amaretti biscuits or sponge fingers
(lady-fingers) (optional)
strawberries or raspberries (optional)

1 Put the egg yolks into a heatproof bowl and whisk until a pale yellow colour, using a rotary, balloon or electric whisk.

2 Whisk in the sugar, followed by the Marsala, continuing to whisk all the time.

3 Stand the bowl over a saucepan of very gently simmering water, or transfer to the top of a double boiler, and continue to whisk until the mixture thickens sufficiently to stand in soft peaks. On no account allow the water to boil or the zabaglione will over-cook and turn into scrambled eggs.

4 Scrape around the sides of the bowl from time to time while whisking. As soon as the mixture is really thick and foamy, take from the heat and continue to whisk for a couple of minutes longer.

5 Pour immediately into stemmed glasses and serve warm; or leave until cold and serve chilled.

6 Fruits such as strawberries or raspberries, or crumbled sponge fingers (lady-fingers) or amaretti biscuits may be placed in the base of the glasses before adding the zabaglione.

Step *1*

Step *2*

Step *4*

Ricotta Ice-Cream

*Ice-cream is a traditional Italian dish, and the numerous flavours are
available usually sold in a cone. However, it is also served sliced.*

SERVES 4-6

INGREDIENTS

30 g/1 oz/¼ cup pistachio nuts
30 g/1 oz/¼ cup walnuts or pecan nuts
30 g/1 oz/¼ cup toasted chopped hazelnuts
grated rind of 1 orange
grated rind of 1 lemon
30 g/1 oz/2 tbsp crystallized or stem ginger
30 g/1 oz/2 tbsp glacé cherries
30 g/1 oz/¼ cup dried apricots
30 g/1 oz/3 tbsp raisins
500 g/1 lb/1½ cups Ricotta
2 tbsp Maraschino, Amaretto or brandy
1 tsp vanilla essence
4 egg yolks
125 g/4 oz/½ cup caster (superfine) sugar

TO DECORATE

whipped cream
a few glacé cherries, pistachio nuts
or mint leaves

1 Roughly chop the pistachio nuts and walnuts and mix with the toasted hazelnuts, orange and lemon rind. Finely chop the ginger, cherries, apricots and raisins, and add to the bowl.

2 Stir the Ricotta evenly through the fruit mixture, then beat in the liqueur and vanilla essence.

3 Put the egg yolks and sugar in a bowl and whisk hard until very thick and creamy – they may be whisked over a pan of gently simmering water to speed up the process. Leave to cool if necessary.

4 Carefully fold the Ricotta mixture evenly through the beaten eggs and sugar until smooth.

5 Line a 18 × 12 cm/7 × 5 inch loaf tin (pan) with a double layer of clingfilm (plastic wrap) or baking parchment. Pour in the Ricotta mixture, level the top, cover with more clingfilm (plastic wrap) or baking parchment and chill in the freezer until firm – at least overnight.

6 To serve, carefully remove the ice-cream from the tin (pan) and peel off the paper. Place on a serving dish and decorate with whipped cream, glacé cherries, pistachio nuts and/or mint leaves. Serve in slices.

Step *1*

Step *4*

Step *5*

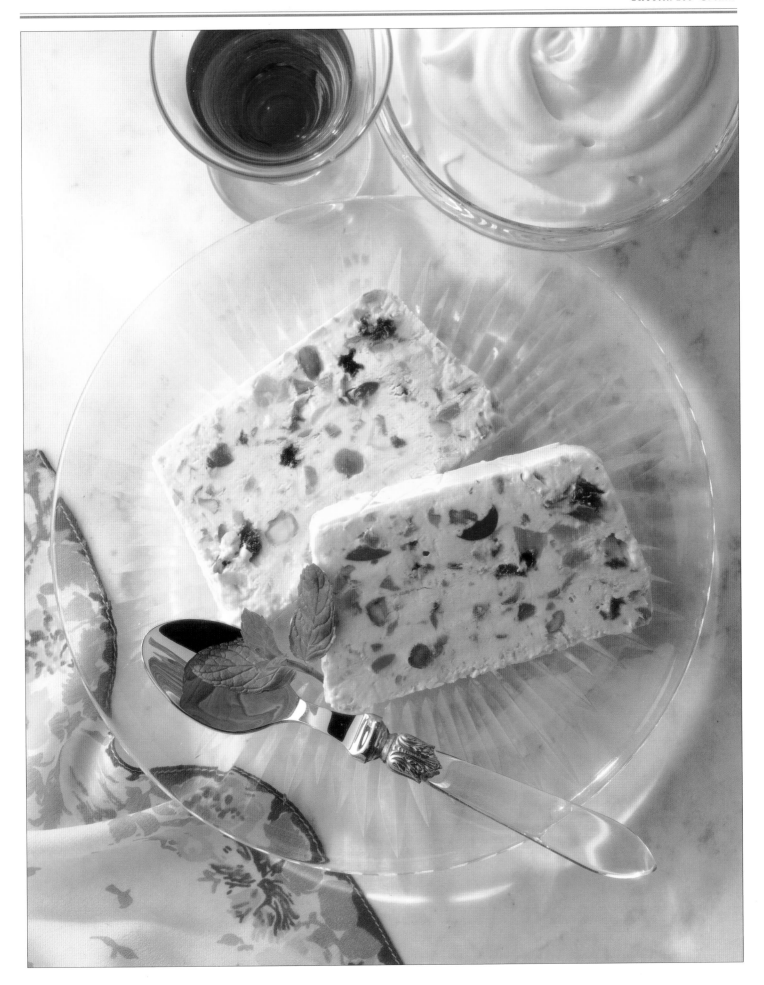

Caramelized Oranges

The secret of these oranges is to allow them to marinate in the syrup for at least 24 hours, so the flavours amalgamate.

SERVES 6

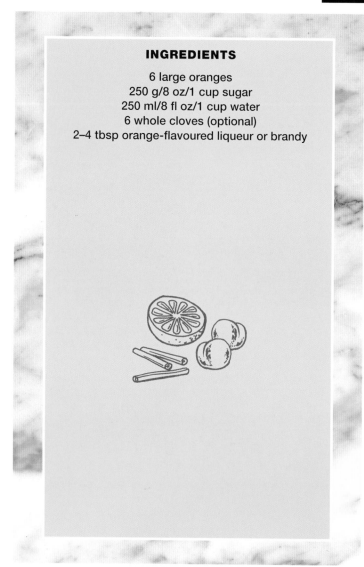

INGREDIENTS

6 large oranges
250 g/8 oz/1 cup sugar
250 ml/8 fl oz/1 cup water
6 whole cloves (optional)
2–4 tbsp orange-flavoured liqueur or brandy

1 Using a citrus zester or potato peeler, pare the rind from two of the oranges in narrow strips without any white pith attached. If using a potato peeler, cut the peel into very thin julienne strips.

2 Put the strips into a small saucepan and barely cover with water. Bring to the boil and simmer for 5 minutes. Drain the strips and reserve the water.

3 Cut away all the white pith and peel from the remaining oranges using a very sharp knife. Then cut horizontally into four slices. Reassemble the oranges and hold in place with wooden cocktail sticks. Stand in a heatproof dish.

4 Put the sugar and water into a heavy-based saucepan with the cloves, if using. Bring to the boil and simmer gently until the sugar has dissolved, then boil hard without stirring until the syrup thickens and begins to colour. Continue to cook until a light golden brown, then quickly remove from the heat and carefully pour in the reserved orange rind liquid.

5 Place over a gentle heat until the caramel has fully dissolved again, then remove from the heat and add the liqueur or brandy. Pour over the oranges.

6 Sprinkle the orange strips over the oranges, cover with clingfilm (plastic wrap) and leave until cold. Chill for at least 3 hours and preferably for 24–48 hours before serving. If time allows, spoon the syrup over the oranges several times while they are marinating. Discard the cocktail stick before serving.

Step *3*

Step *5*

Step *6*

Pear Tart

*Pears are a very popular fruit in Italy. In this recipe from Trentino they
are flavoured with almonds, cinnamon, raisins and apricot jam.*

SERVES 4–6

INGREDIENTS

275 g/9 oz/2¼ cups plain flour
pinch of salt
125 g/4 oz/½ cup caster (superfine) sugar
125 g/4 oz/½ cup butter, diced
1 egg
1 egg yolk
few drops of vanilla essence
2–3 tsp water
sifted icing (confectioners') sugar,
for sprinkling

FILLING

4 tbsp apricot jam
60 g/2 oz amaretti or ratafia biscuits, crumbled
850–1 kg/1¾–2 lb pears, peeled and cored
1 tsp ground cinnamon
90 g/3 oz/½ cup raisins
60 g/2 oz/⅓ cup soft brown or
demerara sugar

1 Sift the flour and salt on to a flat surface, make a well in the centre and add the sugar, butter, egg, egg yolk, vanilla essence and most of the water.

2 Using your fingers gradually work the flour into the other ingredients to give a smooth, pliable dough, adding a little more water if necessary. Wrap in clingfilm (plastic wrap) and chill for an hour or until firm. Alternatively, put all the ingredients into a food processor and process until evenly blended and smooth.

3 Roll out about three-quarters of the dough and use to line a shallow 25 cm/10 inch cake tin or deep flan tin. Spread the apricot jam over the base and sprinkle with the crushed biscuits.

4 Slice the pears very thinly. Arrange over the biscuits in the pastry case. Sprinkle first with cinnamon then with raisins, and finally with the brown sugar.

5 Roll out a thin sausage shape using about one-third of the remaining dough, and place around the edge of the pie. Roll the remainder into thin sausages and arrange in a lattice over the pie, 4 or 5 strips in each direction, attaching them to the strip around the edge.

6 Cook in a preheated oven, 200°C/400°F/Gas Mark 6, for about 50 minutes until golden brown and cooked through. Remove from the oven and leave to cool. Serve warm or chilled, sprinkled with sifted icing (confectioners') sugar.

Step *1*

Step *3*

Step *5*

Panforte di Siena

*This famous Tuscan honey and nut cake is a Christmas speciality. In Italy
it is sold in pretty boxes, and served in very thin slices.*

SERVES 12

INGREDIENTS

125 g/4 oz/1 cup split whole almonds
125 g/4 oz/³⁄₄ cup hazelnuts
90 g/3 oz/¹⁄₂ cup cut mixed peel
60 g/2 oz/¹⁄₃ cup no-soak dried apricots
60 g/2 oz glacé or crystallized pineapple
grated rind of 1 large orange
60 g/2 oz/¹⁄₂ cup plain (all-purpose) flour
2 tbsp cocoa powder
2 tsp ground cinnamon
125 g/4 oz/¹⁄₂ cup caster (superfine) sugar
175 g/6 oz/¹⁄₂ cup honey
icing (confectioners') sugar, for dredging

1 Toast the almonds under the grill (broiler) until lightly browned and place in a bowl. Toast the hazelnuts until the skins split. Place on a dry tea towel (dish cloth) and rub off the skins. Roughly chop the hazelnuts and add to the almonds with the mixed peel.

2 Chop the apricots and pineapple fairly finely, add to the nuts with the orange rind and mix well.

3 Sift the flour with the cocoa and cinnamon, add to the nut mixture and mix evenly.

4 Line a round 20 cm/8 inch cake tin or deep loose-based flan tin with baking parchment.

5 Put the sugar and honey into a saucepan and heat until the sugar dissolves, then boil gently for about 5 minutes or until the mixture thickens and begins to turn a deeper shade of brown. Quickly add to the nut mixture and mix evenly. Turn into the prepared tin and level the top using the back of a damp spoon.

6 Cook in a preheated oven, 150°C/300°F/Gas Mark 2, for 1 hour. Remove from the oven and leave in the tin until cold. Take out of the tin and carefully peel off the paper. Before serving, dredge the cake heavily with sifted icing (confectioners') sugar. Serve in very thin slices.

Step *1*

Step *2*

Step *5*

INDEX

A

Abruzzi 8
Alaska pizza 220
almonds:
    panforte di Siena 252
American hot chilli beef pizza 208
anchovies:
    herbed onion pizza with
      anchovies 222
    tuna, bean and anchovy salad 36
anelli 10
antipasti 19–44
Apulia 9
artichokes:
    artichoke and Parma ham
      (prosciutto) salad 32
    Mediterranean spaghetti 108
    pan-cooked chicken with
      artichokes 138
    three cheese and artichoke
      pizza 238
artichokes, Jerusalem
    see Jerusalem artichokes
aubergines (eggplant):
    aubergine and lamb pizza 214
    aubergine cake 76
    aubergine salad 40
    baked aubergine Parma-style 44
    baked aubergines with pasta 106
    courgette (zucchini) and
      aubergine lasagne 110
    Mediterranean spaghetti 108
    Sicilian spaghetti 84
avocado and ham pizza 204

B

bacon:
    beef olives in rich gravy 152
    breakfast pizza 210
    layered meat loaf 74
    smoky bacon and peperoni
      pizza 200
    spaghetti carbonara 62
baked aubergine (eggplant)
    Parma-style 44
baked aubergines (eggplant) with
    pasta 106
baked beans:
    breakfast pizza 210
baked fennel gratinati 42
baked sea bass 126
barbecued chicken 140
basil:
    pesto 48
    warm pasta with basil
      vinaigrette 38
Basilicata 9

bass *see sea bass*
béchamel sauce 13
beef:
    American hot chilli beef
      pizza 208
    beef in Barolo 150
    beef olives in rich gravy 152
    layered meat loaf 74
    pasticcio 78
    pizzaiola steak 148
    Sicilian spaghetti 84
    spaghetti Bolognese 66
    spicy meatball pizza 206
    tagliatelle with meatballs 68
bell peppers *see peppers*
biscuit (scone) base, pizzas 188
bozzoli 10
bread:
    crostini alla Fiorentina 34
    French bread pizzas 228
bread dough base 186
breakfast pizza 210
bucatini 10

C

Calabria 9
Calabrian pizza 198
calf's liver:
    liver with wine sauce 158
calzone 202
Campania 8–9
cannellini beans:
    minestrone with pesto 48
cannelloni, stuffed 72
capers:
    skewered monkfish with
      caper sauce 132
cappelletti 10
cappelli d'angelo 10
cappellini 10
caramelized oranges 248
casareccia 10
casseroles and stews:
    beef in Barolo 150
    lamb with olives 162
    lazy polenta with rabbit
      stew 178
    squid and macaroni stew 102
    squid casserole 124
cavatappi 10
cheese, 14
    aubergine (eggplant) cake 76
    Calabrian pizza 198
    cheese sauce 14
    courgette (zucchini) and
      aubergine (eggplant)
      lasagne 110

French bread pizzas 228
    gnocchi Romana 172
    Mozzarella in carozza 24
    pesto 48
    pizzas 17
    Ricotta ice-cream 246
    roasted vegetable and goat's
      cheese pizza 224
    spinach and Ricotta gnocchi 174
    stuffed cannelloni 72
    three cheese and artichoke
      pizza 238
    tricolour timballini 112
chicken:
    barbecued chicken 140
    chicken scallops 144
    chicken with green olives 142
    pan-cooked chicken with
      artichokes 138
    Roman chicken 146
    tagliatelle with chicken sauce 64
    tortellini 82
chillies:
    American hot chilli beef
      pizza 208
    spicy meatball pizza 206
clam sauce, vermicelli with 92
cod:
    steamed pasta pudding 88
    see also smoked cod
coffee:
    tiramisu 242
conchiglie 10
conchigliette 10
cornetti 10
cornmeal *see polenta*
courgette (zucchini) and aubergine
    (eggplant) lasagne 110
cream cheese, tiramisu 242
cream of artichoke soup 52
cresti di gallo 10
crostini alla Fiorentina 34

D

desserts 241-52
ditali 10
dough:
    bread dough base 186
    pasta 11
    pizza 15, 16
dressing, French 32
dumplings *see gnocchi*

E

eggplant *see aubergines*
eggs:
    Calabrian pizza 198

Florentine pizza 218
    spaghetti carbonara 62
eliche 10
elicoidali 10
Emilia-Romagna 8

F

farfalle 10
fedeli 10
fennel gratinati 42
festonati 10
fettuccine 10
fiochette 10
fish 123-34
    fish soup 56
    steamed pasta pudding 88
    see also cod; monkfish etc
flan, vermicelli 120
Florentine pizza 218
flour, for pizza dough 16
four seasons pizza 196
freezing:
    pasta 12
    pizzas 17
French bread pizzas 228
French dressing 32
French (green) beans:
    tuna, bean and anchovy salad 36
frezine 10
funny faces pizza 212
fusilli 10
    layered meat loaf 74
    pasticcio 78
fusilli bucati 10

G

garlic:
    baked sea bass 126
    garlic mayonnaise 30
    green garlic tagliatelle 104
    pan-fried prawns (shrimp)
      with garlic 134
    pesto 48
    potato gnocchi with garlic and
      herb sauce 170
gemelli 10
    pasta with green vegetable
      sauce 116
giardiniera pizza 230
gnocchi:
    gnocchi Romana 172
    potato gnocchi with garlic
      and herb sauce 170
    spinach and Ricotta gnocchi 174
goat's cheese:
    roasted vegetable and goat's
      cheese pizza 224

gramigna *10*
green beans *see French beans*
green garlic tagliatelle *104*

H
ham:
   avocado and ham pizza *204*
   calzone *202*
   see also Parma ham
haricot beans:
   haricot bean and pasta soup *54*
   vegetarian pasta and bean
      casserole *118*
hazelnuts:
   panforte di Siena *252*
herbed onion pizza with
   anchovies *222*
herbs, pizzas *17*
honey:
   panforte di Siena *252*

I
ice-cream, Ricotta *246*

J
Jerusalem artichokes:
   cream of artichoke soup *52*

K
kebabs:
   skewered monkfish with
      caper sauce *132*
kidney beans *see red kidney beans*
kneading pizza dough *16*

L
lamb:
   aubergine (eggplant) and lamb
      pizza *214*
   aubergine (eggplant) cake *76*
   lamb sauce *13*
   lamb with olives *162*
   pot roasted leg of lamb *160*
lasagne *10*
   courgette (zucchini) and
      aubergine (eggplant)
      lasagne *110*
   lasagne verde *70*
   seafood lasagne *100*
layered meat loaf *74*
Lazio *8*
lazy polenta with rabbit stew *178*
lentils:
   ratatouille and lentil pizza *234*
Liguria *8*
linguini *10*
liver:
   crostini alla Fiorentina *34*
   liver with wine sauce *158*
Lombardy *6*
lumache *10*
lumachine *11*

M
macaroni *11*

chicken scallops *144*
   macaroni and prawn (shrimp)
      bake *98*
   squid and macaroni stew *102*
   steamed pasta pudding *88*
maccheroni *11*
maltagliati *11*
mangetout (snow peas):
   tofu (bean curd) pizza with
      sweetcorn and peas *236*
marinara pizza *216*
Marsala:
   zabaglione *244*
Mascarpone cheese:
   tiramisu *242*
mayonnaise, garlic *30*
meat and poultry dishes *137–66*
   preserved meats (salumi) *22*
   see also beef; lamb etc
meat loaf, layered *74*
meatballs:
   spicy meatball pizza *206*
   tagliatelle with meatballs *68*
Mediterranean (bell) pepper
   salad *20*
Mediterranean spaghetti *108*
Milanese risotto *180*
minestrone with pesto *48*
mixed (bell) peppers and red
   onion pizza *226*
Molise *8*
monkfish:
   skewered monkfish with caper
      sauce *132*
mortadella ham:
   calzone *202*
Mozzarella *14, 17*
   Calabrian pizza *198*
   Mozzarella in carozza *24*
mushrooms:
   breakfast pizza *210*
   green garlic tagliatelle *104*
   polenta *176*
   spaghetti carbonara *62*
   vermicelli flan *120*
   wild mushroom and walnut
      pizza *232*
mussels:
   mussels in white wine *58*
   pasta shells with mussels *90*

N
noodles *see tagliatelle*
nuts:
   Ricotta ice-cream *246*
   see also almonds; walnuts etc

O
oil, pizza dough *16*
olive oil *14*
olives:
   black olive pâté *26*
   chicken with green olives *142*
   French bread pizzas *228*
   lamb with olives *162*

pork fillet stuffed with
   prosciutto *166*
   Roman chicken *146*
onions:
   herbed onion pizza with
      anchovies *222*
   mixed (bell) peppers and red
      onion pizza *226*
oranges, caramelized *248*
orecchiette *11*
orzi *11*

P
pan-cooked chicken with
   artichokes *138*
pan-fried prawns (shrimp) with
   garlic *134*
panforte di Siena *252*
pappardelle *11*
Parma ham (prosciutto):
   artichoke and Parma ham
      salad *32*
   baked aubergine (eggplant)
      Parma-style *44*
   Mozzarella in carozza *24*
   pork fillet stuffed with
      prosciutto *166*
   saltimbocca *154*
Parmesan *14*
parsley:
   spaghetti with tuna and parsley
      sauce *96*
pasta *10–14, 61–120*
   basic dough *11*
   cooking *12*
   freezing *12*
   nutritional value *11*
   pasta all'uovo *10*
   quantities to serve *12*
   sauces for *13–14*
   storing *12*
   varieties *10–11*
   see also lasagne; spaghetti etc
pasta machines *12*
pasta shapes:
   aubergine (eggplant) cake *76*
   haricot bean and pasta soup *54*
   pasta with green vegetable
      sauce *116*
   warm pasta with basil
      vinaigrette *38*
pasta shells:
   pasta shells with mussels *90*
   vegetable pasta stir-fry *114*
pasticcio *78*
pâté, black olive *26*
pearlini *11*
pear tart *250*
peas, rice and *182*
Pecorino *14*
penne *11*
baked aubergines (eggplant) with
   pasta *106*
vegetarian pasta and bean
   casserole *118*

peperoni:
   smoky bacon and peperoni
      pizza *200*
peppers:
   Calabrian pizza *198*
   Mediterranean (bell) pepper
      salad *20*
   mixed (bell) peppers and red
      onion pizza *226*
   roast (bell) pepper salad *28*
   Roman chicken *146*
   tomato and pepper sauce *24*
pesto, minestrone with *48*
Piedmont *6*
pine kernels (nuts):
   pesto *48*
pipe rigate *11*
pizzaiola steak *148*
pizzas *15–17, 185–238*
   Alaska *220*
   American hot chilli beef *208*
   aubergine (eggplant) and
      lamb *214*
   avocado and ham *204*
   bread dough base *186*
   breakfast *210*
   Calabrian *198*
   calzone *202*
   dough *15*
   Florentine *218*
   four seasons *196*
   freezing *17*
   French bread *228*
   funny faces *212*
   giardiniera *230*
   herbed onion with
      anchovies *222*
   marinara *216*
   mixed (bell) peppers and red
      onion *226*
   potato base *190*
   ratatouille and lentil *234*
   roasted vegetable and goat's
      cheese *224*
   scone (biscuit) base *188*
   smoky bacon and peperoni *200*
   spicy meatball *206*
   three cheese and artichoke *238*
   tofu (bean curd) with sweetcorn
      and peas *236*
   toppings *16–17*
   wild mushroom and walnut *232*
polenta *176*
   lazy polenta with rabbit
      stew *178*
pork:
   pork chops with sage *164*
   pork fillet stuffed with
      prosciutto *166*
pot roasted leg of lamb *160*
potatoes:
   potato base for pizzas *190*
   potato gnocchi with garlic and
      sauce *170*
   sardine and potato bake *130*

poultry and meat dishes *137-66*
prawns (shrimp):
    macaroni and prawn (shrimp)
      bake *98*
    pan-fried prawns (shrimp) with
      garlic *134*
    spaghetti with seafood sauce *86*
preserved meats (salumi) *22*
prosciutto *see Parma ham*
Puglia *9*
pumpkin, tagliatelle with *80*

R

rabbit stew, lazy polenta with *178*
ragû:
    lasagne verde *70*
    spaghetti Bolognese *66*
ratatouille and lentil pizza *234*
red kidney beans:
    American hot chilli beef
      pizza *208*
    red bean soup *50*
ribbon noodles *see tagliatelle*
rice:
    Milanese risotto *180*
    rice and peas *182*
Ricotta *14*
    Calabrian pizza *198*
    Ricotta ice-cream *246*
    spinach and Ricotta gnocchi *174*
rigatoni *11*
risotto, Milanese *180*
roast (bell) pepper salad *28*
roasted vegetable and goat's cheese
    pizza *224*
Roman chicken *146*
ruoti *11*

S

sage:
    pork chops with sage *164*
    saltimbocca *154*
salads:
    artichoke and Parma ham
      (prosciutto) *32*
    aubergine (eggplant) *40*
    Mediterranean (bell) pepper *20*
    roast (bell) pepper *28*
    seafood *30*
    tuna, bean and anchovy *36*
salami:
    Calabrian pizza *198*
    calzone *202*
salmon:
    Alaska pizza *220*
    see also smoked salmon
salt, pizza dough *16*
saltimbocca *154*
salumi *22*
sardine and potato bake *130*
Sardinia *9*
sauces:
    béchamel *13*
    cheese *14*
    chicken *64*

for pasta *13-14*
    garlic *126*
    green vegetable *116*
    lamb *13*
    mushroom *176*
    special tomato *194*
    tomato *13, 16–17, 192*
    tomato and pepper *24*
sausages:
    breakfast pizza *210*
scone (biscuit) base, pizzas *188*
sea bass, baked *126*
seafood:
    marinara pizza *216*
    seafood lasagne *100*
    seafood salad *30*
    spaghetti with seafood sauce *86*
semini *11*
semolina:
    gnocchi Romana *172*
shrimp *see prawns*
Sicilian spaghetti *84*
Sicily *9*
skewered monkfish with caper
    sauce *132*
smoked cod:
    seafood lasagne *100*
smoked salmon, spaghetti with *94*
smoky bacon and peperoni
    pizza *200*
snow peas *see mangetout*
soups *47–58*
    cream of artichoke *52*
    fish *56*
    haricot bean and pasta *54*
    minestrone with pesto *48*
    mussels in white wine *58*
    red bean *50*
spaghetti *11*
    Mediterranean spaghetti *108*
    Sicilian spaghetti *84*
    spaghetti Bolognese *66*
    spaghetti carbonara *62*
    spaghetti with seafood
      sauce *86*
    spaghetti with smoked
      salmon *94*
    spaghetti with tuna and parsley
      sauce *96*
    tricolour timballini *112*
special tomato sauce *194*
spicy meatball pizza *206*
spinach:
    Florentine pizza *218*
    green garlic tagliatelle *104*
    spinach and Ricotta gnocchi *174*
    stuffed cannelloni *72*
spirale *11*
squid:
    squid and macaroni stew *102*
    squid casserole *124*
steak, pizzaiola *148*
steamed pasta pudding *88*
stews *see casseroles and stews*
storing pasta *12*

strozzapreti *11*
stuffed cannelloni *72*
sweetcorn, tofu (bean curd) pizza
    with peas and *236*

T

tagliarini *11*
tagliatelle *11*
    green garlic tagliatelle *104*
    tagliatelle with chicken sauce *64*
    tagliatelle with meatballs *68*
    tagliatelle with pumpkin *80*
tart, pear *250*
three cheese and artichoke
    pizza *238*
timballini, tricolour *112*
tiramisu *242*
toasts, tomato *20*
tofu (bean curd) pizza with
    sweetcorn and peas *236*
tomatoes:
    baked aubergine (eggplant)
      Parma-style *44*
    baked aubergines (eggplant)
      with pasta *106*
    basic tomato sauce *13*
    Calabrian pizza *198*
    French bread pizzas *228*
    pizzaiola steak *148*
    special tomato sauce *194*
    tomato and pepper sauce *24*
    tomato sauce *16–17, 192*
    tomato toasts *20*
toppings, pizza *16–17*
tortellini *82*
tortiglione *11*
Trentino-Alto Adige *6*
tricolour timballini *112*
trout in red wine *128*
tuna:
    spaghetti with tuna and parsley
      sauce *96*
    tuna, bean and anchovy salad *36*
    vitello tonnato *156*
Tuscany *8*

U

Umbria/Marches *8*

V

veal:
    saltimbocca *154*
    vitello tonnato *156*
vegetables:
    giardiniera pizza *230*
    minestrone with pesto *48*
    pasta with green vegetable
      sauce *116*
    roasted vegetable and goat's
      cheese pizza *224*
    vegetable pasta stir-fry *114*
vegetarian pasta and bean
    casserole *118*
Veneto *6–8*
vermicelli *11*

vermicelli flan *120*
vermicelli with clam sauce *92*
vinaigrette, basil *38*
vitello tonnato *156*

W

walnuts:
    wild mushroom and walnut
      pizza *232*
water, pizza dough *16*
wild mushroom and walnut
    pizza *232*
wine:
    beef in Barolo *150*
    liver with wine sauce *158*
    mussels in white wine *58*
    trout in red wine *128*

Y

yeast *15–16*
yogurt:
    pasticcio *78*

Z

zabaglione *244*
ziti tagliati *11*
zucchini *see courgettes*